Lil' Red

A Story of Survival, Healing, and Forgiveness

JILL SAFARI

LANDON
HAIL
PRESS

Copyright© 2025 Jill Safari
All Rights Reserved

This book or any portion thereof may not be reproduced or used in any manner without the express written permission of the publisher, except for the use of brief quotations in a book review.

Paperback ISBN: 978-1-959955-60-3
Hardback ISBN: 978-1-959955-61-0

Cover design by Jill Safari, Jake Gardiner, Klonism Art and Design, and Rich Johnson, Spectacle Photo
Published by Landon Hail Press

Although the author and publisher have made every effort to ensure the accuracy and completeness of information contained in this book, we assume no responsibility for errors, inaccuracies, omissions, or any inconsistency herein. Any slights on people, places, or organizations are unintentional. The material in this book is provided for educational purposes only. No responsibility for loss occasioned to any person or corporate body acting or refraining to act as a result of reading material in this book can be accepted by the author or publisher.

This book is dedicated to:

My daughters, who inspire me to be
my best self, living my best life every day.

My husband, my partner in all things,
my best friend, my everything.
With you by my side, I really *can* do anything.

My sisters, born and chosen, who have
looked over me, stood beside me, guided,
supported, encouraged and loved me.

And to all the victims who are suffering
or have suffered from bullying and abuse,
those who don't have a voice but desperately need to be
heard.

Contents

Introduction: Lil' Red vs. The Wolves ___ 1

PART ONE: The Little Wolves ___ 7
Chapter 1: The Life Force ___ 9
Chapter 2: The Unicorn ___ 17
Chapter 3: The Adventurer ___ 26
Chapter 4: The Fighter ___ 31

PART TWO: The Mama and Papa Wolves ___ 41
Chapter 5: Attachments ___ 43
Chapter 6: The Heat of Anger ___ 49
Chapter 7: Absent Papa Wolf ___ 57
Chapter 8: Forgiveness ___ 64
Chapter 9: A New School Culture ___ 70
Chapter 10: Broadening Horizons ___ 75
Chapter 11: Finding My Voice ___ 83
Chapter 12: Looking Back ___ 93

PART THREE: The Big, Bad Wolf ___ 99
Chapter 13: Teasing the Wolf ___ 101
Chapter 14: Life Shifts ___ 106
Chapter 15: The Tables Are Turned ___ 113
Chapter 16: Joy Unravels ___ 120
Chapter 17: Portland ___ 131
Chapter 18: Beginning of the End ___ 135

Chapter 19: Do or Die	139
Chapter 20: On the Run	144
Chapter 21: Finally Free	148
PART FOUR: The She-Wolf	**155**
Chapter 22: Her Spirit	157
Chapter 23: Her Den	168
Chapter 24: Her Pack	179
Chapter 25: Her Cubs	182
Chapter 26: Her Courage	189
PART FIVE: Let's Talk More About It	**201**
Part 1 – The Little Wolves: Bullying	203
Part 2 - The Mama & Papa Wolves: Parental Abuse	205
Part 3 - The Big, Bad Wolf: Domestic Violence	208
Part 4 - The She-Wolf: Strong and Resilient	212
Acknowledgments	216
About the Author	218

Introduction

Lil' Red vs. The Wolves

AS I LAY, CURLED into a ball on the dirty, rough carpet, I could feel my bleeding lip swell and the pulsing pain on my cheek. Everywhere hurt. I lay there in the dark, thinking, *This is it*. I was pretty sure I was not going to live until morning. There was no furniture in the room, no lights, nothing. Just a closet and a small above-grade window that led to the alley behind our apartment.

The window that might just save me.

It's hard for any of us to imagine this kind of pain, let alone that it could be caused by someone close to you, someone you *chose* to be with, someone you trusted with your heart and soul. Why is it that our society is so intrigued by violence committed by the hands of mass murderers, rapists, and killers? It is analyzed, documented, even dramatized on television.

But when it's domestic violence, something that occurs between two people who know each other intimately, it suddenly becomes a "private matter." It is something that makes people uncomfortable. Something that makes people turn a blind eye. That is exactly why I've chosen to share *my* story, *Lil' Red*, to bring the darkness of domestic violence and abuse into the light.

This is the story of my journey as an energetic, rambunctious, spirited little red-headed soul, born into a hostile world. Armed only with my cloak of curly red hair, my tenacity, and determination, I was unprepared for the battles with the wolves I encountered in life. These wolves included bullies at school, my own parents, and the Big, Bad Wolf I married, who would eventually put me in that dirty, dark room on that floor, where I had to decide in that moment whether to live or die.

As I began my life journey in the evergreen forests of Washington State, full of bold curiosity and confidence and ready for adventure, I found that my Mama and Papa Wolves were only *in disguise* as loving parents. The reality was I experienced rejection, lack of attachment and nurturing, and abuse under the guise of discipline.

Around the age of seven, when we moved to a new forest in Maryland, I encountered the Little Wolves. Those wolves were disguised as innocent kids, but they were actually fiercely cruel in their relentless bullying. They ostracized and tormented me daily.

Just when it seemed I was doomed to become one of the wolves myself, full of rage and frustration caused by the actions of those around me, our family moved from Maryland to the Black Forest of Munich, Germany, where I would be granted relief from the bullying. Unfortunately, the abuse at home continued.

With my newfound bravery tucked loosely in my pocket and armed with a new sense of confidence and independence, I forged ahead into the age of self-

Introduction

exploration and discovery, otherwise known as adolescence. Upon our family's return to the forests of Washington, I found myself in the midst of turmoil and upheaval. I had a drastic change in living circumstances after the age of sixteen, something that would have a deep and lasting effect on me.

Just around the next bend lurked a Big, Bad Wolf disguised as a loving, supportive, charming, and affectionate partner. It became apparent, however, that this wolf wanted to devour me completely, after inflicting the most horrific pain and suffering.

Writing down my feelings and experiences in those moments of pain and despair, some in great detail, was therapeutic and cathartic for me, as the author, but may be disturbing to you, the reader. As they should be.

Before getting eaten by the wolves in my life, I saved myself and spent years healing through counseling, group therapy, and rebuilding my life one block at a time. You'll also read about how I let go of the hope of a different past and created a better life for myself, eventually proving it was possible to break the cycle of violence with my own children, through determination, education, and a steadfast dedication to unconditional love.

I will share with you how my realization that the very traits I was admonished for throughout my childhood ended up being the same qualities I have relied on in my life to overcome hardship and face adversity. I delve into why I believe we don't get to choose the moments in life that make us who we are. We only choose what we learn from them and what we will carry with us or leave behind.

As you read, you will likely feel what I felt, and you'll see Lil' Red's experiences through her eyes and point of view. You'll also relish in her victories, her strength, her perseverance, and determination. You might even laugh along with her, too. And hopefully, you'll be inspired by her bravery.

Some parts of my story may very well be disturbing to you. It may evoke feelings of sympathy or empathy, sadness, joy, tension, anger, and outrage. Please rest assured, if you can relate to the abuse, you are not alone. I'm not sugarcoating it here–domestic violence is ugly.

Perhaps my story will inspire you, move you, motivate you, or at the least make you pause and ponder the actions of those around you. I hope this story compels you to be more kind, less judgmental, and more understanding and accepting of others—we never know what someone might be going through or what hardships they've endured.

I hope this book encourages you to search for your own peace, contentment, and happiness, to accept nothing less than your best self, your best life. I hope you are encouraged to heal from the pain and trauma of your past, to clean out your emotional closets, and to seek forgiveness for yourself and others, as I did.

And most importantly, if you're experiencing any of the same abuse in any form, I urge you to reach out to someone for help. I have provided a section at the end of the book that has more information on how and where to reach out for help, as well as warning signs for potential wolves in your own life.

Writing my story required an intense commitment to reliving the past and reviving memories of deep pain and suffering, as well as joy, love, adventure, and triumph. These are the words Lil' Red tried so hard to say for many years, when no one would listen.

Introduction

This is my way of shedding much-needed light on still taboo issues in our society, which continue to prevail, despite improvements in laws to protect victims and programs to support both victims and abusers.

It's time for action and time for change.

This is my story.

Lil' Red

PART ONE
The Little Wolves

The lotus flower, in order to bloom, can push its way up six feet through the mud in which it is deeply rooted, continually reemerging with unwavering faith, perseverance, and a fascinating will to live. It is a symbol of life's ebbs and flows, of renewal, grace, self-enlightenment, and rebirth.

Lil' Red

Part One: The Little Wolves

Chapter 1

The Life Force

ON A TYPICALLY OVERCAST, drizzly spring day near the end of April, back in 1965, high up on Seattle's Queen Anne Hill, a young woman was in labor with her second child. As was the tradition at that time, her husband was not by her side. She already had a beautiful daughter who had just turned two, and she was excited to welcome her second child to the world. She thought everything was fine, until she saw the look on the doctor's face as he entered the room.

The doctor came in and informed her that the baby was breech and she could not deliver naturally, so they would need to prep her for an emergency C-section.

She was suddenly gripped with fear and worry. Would her baby be okay? Would *she* be okay?

As panic set in and they were preparing her for surgery, the doctor abruptly stopped everything. Having checked her again, he stated that the baby had, inexplicably and miraculously, turned back around, and they could proceed with the natural birth as planned. It should be noted that this was no small feat for a baby in utero at this stage in the game, but, true to my personality, I was just checking to make sure there wasn't another more efficient way out.

A few hours later, after I'd decided it was, in fact, the best way, a bright, redheaded, blue-eyed, milky-skinned little girl burst her way into the world.

I was told that, when I was born and, to everyone's surprise, popped out with bright-red hair, the doctor blurted out, "Oh, no, there's trouble!" That exclamation set the tone for what seemed to be a general opinion of me throughout most of my childhood: that I was a troublemaker.

I was gifted with a wonderful combination of a mischievous, curious, feisty, adventurous, and highly energetic, rambunctious nature along with my curly red locks. It seemed, though, that my sweet, beautiful soul was born into a bit of a hostile world.

This started with my mother, who was immediately put off by me, whether because of her own personal experience with redheads or because of some antiquated social stereotype, I don't know. Maybe she was still reeling from the drama of my pre-birth acrobatics. For whatever reason, it seems I rubbed her the wrong way from birth. That, too, would be my destiny—to rub people, kids mostly, the wrong way and to be misjudged based on appearance.

To my mother's chagrin, I wasn't anything like my sister. My guess is she was expecting another sweet, compliant, well-mannered little girl like she already had and like most girls in the sixties, but I was far from that. I mean, everything is all about expectations, right? I don't think my father had a strong feeling either way, he was so engrossed in his basic training for the Army and spending

Part One: The Little Wolves

most of his time away from us so was largely unaffected by my arrival.

My sister certainly welcomed me with open arms, though. In her words, I was born with a "palpable energy, a force." She said I had "squishy marshmallow cheeks and legs." She was only two, so for her, I must have seemed like her very own live doll to care for and love.

I did feel my extended family was generally accepting of me, although we rarely saw them. I especially enjoyed the time around my paternal grandmother, because she favored me, since, as she liked to say, she was the one who gave me my red hair. Of course, science would argue that the red hair gene must come from both sides, but no one ever disputed the point with her. She, too, had curly red hair pretty much up until she died at the age of ninety-two (the last several years, she wore a wig, but it was still her).

I was also close to my great-grandfather, Jackson, we called him Grandpa, on my mother's side who gave me the nickname Lil' Red. He always greeted me warmly with big welcoming hugs and an invitation to come sit on his lap. He usually had a shiny, silver fifty-cent piece for me from his pocket whenever we visited him and my great-grandmother, Gammy, and their little white poodle mix, Taffy. I still have one of them, and to this day I carry it around in my purse. I always felt so welcome, loved, and safe whenever I was with them.

My memories of our visits to their house are some of my best memories from childhood. When we were there, things just felt different. Our whole family dynamic was different. I know my mother was close to them, too. They had practically raised her, and even she was a different person when we were there. It was calmer there, more peaceful. My dad was in the military so we moved around a lot, but theirs was a consistent home for us, a haven to retreat to periodically. For me, it also meant a break from being constantly in trouble. It was a place where we were all free to just *be*.

Gammy and Grandpa lived in an old house up in northern Washington State, in Bellingham, where a lot of our extended family on my mother's side also lived. Whenever we visited there, we also spent time with aunts, uncles, cousins, and my grandmother, as well. This was heaven for me. I am definitely a family-oriented person, so, it was always hard for me to cope with living far away from extended family during most of my childhood. These visits gave me the connection to family that I craved.

Gammy was tiny but strong, a gritty woman standing just under five feet tall. She was born in Nebraska in the year 1900. Her given name was Orletta Mae, and she was supposedly part Native American, but we never knew any more details beyond that. The family story was that she had traveled to Washington State in a covered wagon. She married my great-grandfather when she was eighteen, lived through two World Wars, the Depression, the Spanish Flu, and a number of other wars; she gave birth to four children and endured many additional hardships throughout her life. The evidence of a hard life was written in her worn, weathered face. She had long, wiry, black hair heavily peppered with gray that she almost always wore tied up tight in a bun, except when she let it down to brush it at night. She was stingy with her smiles, but on the occasion when she shared one with you, it was a warm, sweet, playful smile.

Part One: The Little Wolves

Grandpa was equally sturdy, his toughness forged by his many years of service as a postal carrier, in addition to living through those same historical events and hardships. He had a quiet confidence and strength and generally wore a warm, affectionate smile on his face. He was passionate about his garden, which occupied most of their large property, and the lushly landscaped yard he worked for many years to create. Besides the calm, welcoming tranquility of their home, the outdoor space was just as much a part of the appeal of their home for me, something I enjoyed immensely during our time with them.

Gammy and Grandpa had four children, the oldest being my grandmother, Barbara Jean (Grandma Jean to us), whom I wasn't especially close to. She worked in a fancy department store called The Bon Marché. My mother would dress the three of us kids up in our Sunday best, and we would go visit her at the store, where we'd be allowed to pick out a special candy as a treat. My mom would get fancied up, too, with her teased beehive hairdo and coordinated outfit that usually included a matching hat. She'd been the beauty queen in high school and was quite lovely in an understated kind of way. Even as a young girl, I always felt so elegant and sophisticated on those outings.

Whenever we stayed at Gammy and Grandpa's house, my siblings and I got to sleep up in the attic together. We loved it up there, all on our own, far away from the adults. We'd giggle, talk and tell stories until we finally fell asleep. As many old houses do, theirs had a back staircase leading down from the attic to the kitchen that felt like a secret passage to us. There was also a huge screened-in front porch where I loved to sit on the cushioned bench and play or just daydream. My absolute favorite spot, though, was their back garden. The huge backyard garden was full of apple trees, with rows and rows of all different vegetables, varieties of berries, and even rabbits in cages. I loved climbing up into one of the apple trees, soaking in the smell of the tart green apples, and then finding my way up into the perfect spot to nestle down where I could sit and eat apples until I was literally sick to my stomach. Then, I would slide down and curl up on the porch swing, swaying back and forth under the shade of the apple tree until I was lulled to sleep.

I loved wandering through Grandpa's prized garden, picking raspberries and strawberries or vegetables for dinner. They had blackberry bushes, too, and when we picked them, Gammy would bake them into a pie for us. She also used to make strawberry-rhubarb pie, still one of my favorite desserts to this day. I try to make it at least once a year around Father's Day and my dad's birthday, since it was his favorite, too.

I adored playing with those soft little rabbits, they seemed so exotic to me. I'll never forget the moment when I was about nine when I came to understand that the "chicken" we were eating wasn't actually chicken but *rabbit*. Of course, this was their purpose—they weren't put there as pets. That didn't stop me from throwing a fit! I cried and cried and was inconsolable over the thought of those fluffy, sweet rabbits being food! I refused to eat them after that, on principle, of course.

My sister, brother, cousins, and I would play in the garden for hours, usually tag or hide-and-seek. Once when we were playing tag, for whatever reason, we had agreed that the front door was base. When I ran up on the big porch

Part One: The Little Wolves

to touch base, I ended up putting my hand on the sidelight window next to the door, instead. To my own shock and the horror of all the adults inside, my hand went right through the glass.

My instinct was to yank it right back out, which is the opposite of what you're *supposed* to do, but I didn't know that. Somehow, I miraculously came out unscathed by any of the jagged shards of window glass. In fact, this would be one of the rare occasions when my story did *not* end in a trip to the emergency room. This time, after everyone verified that there were, in fact, no deep cuts, I only got a severe scolding.

Gammy often taught us things while we were there, usually traditional things like baking, cooking, or mending. Grandpa was the one who taught us about outside things, mostly gardening, but sometimes about fixing things or doing small repairs, like mending fences or animal cages. They were always very patient and loving as they taught.

On one of our visits, when I was about ten, Gammy offered to teach me to crochet. It was difficult, because I was a lefty, but she figured out that, if she sat in front of me and mirrored the technique, I could easily see what to do. I learned quickly and enjoyed doing it for many years. I was always so grateful for her taking the time to teach me and see past my left-handedness, when the rest of the world seemed so against it. Even at that young age, the full meaning behind her patience and kindness resonated with me.

Toward the end of her life, after Grandpa had been put in a home and passed away, she developed Alzheimer's. Then, at eighty-five, she died a quiet, unassuming death that reflected her life. Hers was the first funeral I went to, and the first dead person I ever saw. I kept thinking she looked like she was just asleep and that, at any moment, she was going to open her eyes, sit up, and maybe ask for a cup of tea.

Her death hit me like a ton of bricks. The loss of her and my great-grandfather, who both had meant so much to me growing up, was devastating.

>She had loved me unconditionally.
>She had accepted me just as I was.
>But she was one of few.

Part One: The Little Wolves

Chapter 2

The Unicorn

AT THE TIME I WAS BORN, only about ten percent of the population was left-handed, so I grew up in a right-hand-dominated world. Frankly, not much has changed today—it's still a very right-hand-dominant world, but now, at least we have scissors that work both ways!

If you add my left handedness to the fact that redheads make up less than two percent of the world's population (outside Ireland, anyway) and the combination of red hair *and* blue eyes occurs in just 0.17%—well, you get a *goddamned unicorn*. Supposedly there are also special things about us gingers, but who knows whether those are just part of the stereotype or if they're real.

Some of the myths include that we're more creative, we think with our right brains, and that we're more verbal and analytical. Supposedly we're also more sensitive to pain and at a greater risk of Parkinson's and endometriosis. Redheads are known for their "fiery tempers" and for being strong-willed, both true in my case.

There are also many little things in the right-handed world that non-lefties take for granted, like coffee mugs

Lil' Red

with the design printed on one side or ladles with the pouring spout facing you—both work properly *only* if you hold them in your right hand. But the majority rules, so we lefties do our best to adapt.

But, growing up, one thing I knew without a doubt—I was definitely different. As a kid, I felt like a salmon swimming upstream. Even simple things like using scissors or sitting at the desks at school were overly challenging, since they were designed for right-handers. But being a lefty was just one of my many life challenges. As I grew from being that dependent, loving, trusting infant, my struggles in life grew, too.

I guarantee you, no one explained all of these special qualities to the kids around me when I was growing up. No one told them there were famous actresses, like Anne Margaret, Lucille Ball, Susan Hayward, and Rita Hayworth (she actually dyed hers red), who made red hair cool and even desirable. No one told *them* it was cool to be different, that being unique is a good thing. All those little wolves knew was I was different from them, from *all* of them. I didn't sound that different, maybe with a little bit of Texas twang left over from our brief time living there. I didn't even look that different (if you set aside the red hair). But so what if I did? Who were they to judge me?

When I was in elementary school, teachers always tried to force me to write with my right hand and accused me of using my left hand just to be difficult. It was so embarrassing to be singled out and forced to make "corrections" in front of the other kids. As I grew, I learned to be ashamed of it. I tried to cover and disguise it whenever I could. I taught myself to do as many things as I could with my right hand.

Part One: The Little Wolves

But not crocheting! That I proudly did with my left!

Unfortunately, I also grew up in a time before unicorns were hip. We were still too young to care about being unique. In just a few short years, everyone would be killing themselves to be as different as they could be, piercing their noses, dyeing their hair purple or black, wearing leather, and going full punk. Or maybe they'd be dancing disco in bell bottoms or styling their hair like Farrah Fawcett. But my peers couldn't even imagine all of what was to come. They just knew that, compared to them, I was an alien.

My curly red hair, combined with constantly being the "new kid" and a lefty, made me a target for bullying and teasing for pretty much all of my early childhood. I wasn't someone who could retreat to the "closet" or hide away my uniqueness like other kids who were bullied and teased for being different. Mine was right out there for everyone to see. I wouldn't realize until much later in life that my crazy red hair and the character traits that came with it were actually my greatest gifts in life. Until then, however, I came to see myself the same way as most everyone around me— with contempt, disregard, and self-loathing.

Although the kids at school were cruel and did not accept me, the adults around me seemed to be quite taken with my curly red locks. Most adults I encountered would comment on my "beautiful red hair," and I would politely utter the requisite, *"Thank you,"* while inside I would be fuming. I was sure they were lying. It absolutely felt like false praise. How could what they were saying be true, when all I ever got was ridicule and abuse? All I knew was it seemed to be more of a curse than anything, because most of the time, I was being teased about my red hair.

Lil' Red

The only other people I knew with red hair were my cousin Shelley and my paternal grandmother, from whom I got my red hair gene—well, one of them, anyway. It made me feel better to be around her, which sadly wasn't often. Living the military life meant we were constantly on the move—somewhere new approximately every two years, like clockwork. This lifestyle wasn't suited to a little red-haired, left-handed kid who stood out like a sore thumb everywhere we went.

One of the last times I can remember feeling the complete freedom of the innocence of childhood, before the heavy bullying began, was when I was six years old. We lived in Washington State for a short time, just about an hour from Bellingham and my great grandparents.

Usually, we lived in army housing, but here we had a regular, civilian house on a large corner lot in a suburb just north of Seattle. I fell in love with it immediately, with its massive back yard full of blackberry bushes surrounded by huge trees. I quickly made friends with Michelle, who lived across the street *on a farm*. They didn't have farms in army housing.

This was so novel and new to me, I spent all my time over there unless I was at school. I loved every minute of helping her with her chores, cleaning animal pens, and feeding all the animals. Her parents marveled at how much time I spent helping, but I did it because I enjoyed being near the animals, not because I had to. I especially enjoyed feeding the cows. If you know me, you know I have a deep love of cows to this day. This is where it all started.

Michelle and I also spent a lot of time riding our bikes around, exploring the nearby neighborhoods, including a large empty lot that was an abandoned building site. We

Part One: The Little Wolves

made forts, picked blackberries on the bushes in our backyard, and laughed until our stomachs hurt. Most of our time was spent outdoors, unless it was raining, as it did often—it was the Pacific Northwest, after all.

Sometimes we ignored the rain and just kept playing. This always brought the wrath of my mom in the form of a severe scolding along with a swift smack on the butt. The message was always the same: I was bad, a troublemaker, and why couldn't I just *behave*? Of course, all the rain also meant we were surrounded by lush, green forests of towering, exquisite pine trees, as well as the many native varieties of deciduous trees. There is also a persistent grayness to the weather in the PNW, as if the world around you is heavy with an unexpressed sadness.

On one of the rare sunny days in early summer, when Michelle and I were out riding our bikes on the dirt and gravel mounds of the abandoned lot, I got going too fast and lost control of my bike. I skidded sideways, and the next thing I knew, I was going head over heels over the handlebars.

I got pretty scraped up from the gravel—road rash they call it—on my arms and legs, but I took the worst of it on my left elbow where I landed. I had an open gash about two inches long and could actually see the bone, which intrigued me more than anything. I was more worried about being in trouble for messing up my bike and clothes than I was about my cut. I knew it meant I was off to the emergency room, someplace that was already too familiar.

My first stitches had come when I was just one and a half. I split open the skin just below my eyebrow when I hit my head on a table. Whether you call it "accident prone," adventurous, curious, or clumsy, that was me. Usually it was just one of my parents who took me in, but this trip would be different. This time, my very best friend, Michelle, came with me and held my other hand while I got stitched up. I'll never forget this small act of bravery and solidarity on her part.

As was always the case, just when I was building a good friendship, we had to move again. It was pointless, but I pitched a fit, crying and yelling at my parents about the unfairness of having to leave Michelle and her farm animals, including my beloved cows. You would have thought they were mine, the way I carried on. I had grown close to those cows, especially the newest calf who'd been recently born and whom we'd named Greg (from the Brady Bunch).

This also meant moving away from my great-grandparents, which was especially hard for me. And since our next move was to the forests of Maryland, we literally could not have moved farther away without leaving the country.

I've often reminisced about my life and wondered how different it might have been had we stayed there in northern Washington where I could be close to my great-grandparents and relished that peaceful, idyllic life in a safe place full of unconditional love and support.

What if...? But we don't always get to choose the moments that define us.

Instead, I found myself being the new kid again and standing out like a sore thumb. The ridicule and embarrassment of my first day at school was only the start, just a small taste of the daily bullying I would experience over the next two years. In Washington State, I had started

Part One: The Little Wolves

to notice being treated differently at school, but here the teasing and bullying kicked into high gear.

Imagine the scene: You're eight years old, and you've already been bullied at school for a couple of years because of your red hair, which you can't do anything about even if you wanted to. You're forced to leave a place you know and love, living near people you love, to move to the other side of the country to a completely new home, school, and life.

You walk into the class halfway through the school year. The kids all know one another, social circles are well-established. The teacher asks you to stand in front of the class and introduce yourself, but before you can get your name out, someone mutters under their breath, "Carrot top." All the kids snicker.

The teacher politely hushes them and tells you to proceed. Now, with your face as red as your hair, you quietly say, "Jill Bohannon." Then, the teacher welcomes you and asks you to take a seat at the empty desk in the back of the classroom.

Awkwardly, you make your way to your seat while other kids gawk at you, whispering things to one another and making snide comments as you pass. You just lower your eyes, fight back the tears, and sit down, grateful to be hidden away in the back.

The teacher then asks all the students to take out a pencil and paper and gives instructions for a simple writing task. The desk is one of those wooden varieties with a chair and small desktop attached to it—*on the right*. You think, *Oh, no, what do I do now?* You decide to roll with it, turning yourself and your paper a bit sideways, then start to write.

The teacher immediately comes over to your desk to ask, "Just what do you think you are doing?"

You look up at her, puzzled by the question, thinking, *I'm writing, like you asked me to.* But instead, you just say, "Writing?"

She says, loud enough for the entire class to hear, "But you're writing upside down and sideways. You must know that is *not* how we write properly. Please turn your paper around and write with the proper hand." More snickering from the other kids, more whispering.

Now what? Shit. You don't know *how* to write with the other hand. So, you ask to be excused to the bathroom instead and go have a good cry. Once you've calmed down enough, you slink back into the class trying to go unnoticed, and slide back into your seat. You fake write with your right hand, and when no one is looking, you quickly finish the assignment with your left. Welcome to second grade. Welcome to the daily life of Lil' Red.

As our family settled into our new home, I found myself sitting alone for lunch most days at school. I pretended it didn't bother me, but it really did. I was already experiencing isolation while eating at home, because my mother forced me to sit at the table alone until bedtime whenever I refused to eat certain foods. Having this negative experience at school, too, wasn't helping me. It would take me well into late adulthood to grow out of my distaste for eating alone.

I also played alone during recess for the most part. I would swing around on the monkey bars or practice my marble shooting alone, except on the rare occasion when a teacher intervened. Occasionally, they would notice I was being left out and force the other kids to include me in a game of four-square, jump rope, or dodgeball.

I know they thought they were doing the right thing, but it never felt very good. It drew attention to my isolation and almost made it worse to force the other kids to include me which made them resent me even more. I would have benefitted so much more from them admonishing the other kids and *teaching* them that what they were doing was wrong. Most of the time though, the teachers either didn't notice or just didn't care that I wasn't included in the playground games. Especially anything where it was left up to the other kids to choose teams. So, I learned to make my own fun, a skill I would develop into a positive trait later in life.

Chapter 3

The Adventurer

DESPITE THE BULLYING, I actually liked school. I already knew that someday, I wanted to be a teacher and I often played imaginary school with my stuffed animals as my students. I loved coming up with little lessons for them. I would talk to them about frogs, cows, building forts, and riding bikes—all the things I knew about and loved. However, real school and my version of school were as different as night and day.

Although I did have a couple of friends who lived on my street in Maryland, I often played alone, same as I did at school. I was either happily wandering out in the woods behind our house, catching frogs, "teaching" school in my room with my stuffed animals or just playing with my toys. We had a vast forest behind our home that was thick with huge oak trees and had a big creek running through it. There was also a beautiful, winding, tree-lined path through the forest that we walked on to and from school.

Catching frogs quickly became one of my favorite pastimes. I spent hours sitting, watching, and waiting for my moment. Then, once I'd caught one, I carefully held my little friend tenderly in cupped hands as I walked back home where I had a terrarium waiting for them, complete with water, rocks, sticks, and leaves—all the things I thought they were used to and had thoughtfully collected. I also caught little bugs for them to eat. I kept them for a few days at a time, and then I would just as carefully and lovingly return them to the very spot where I'd found them. I also used to grow them from tadpoles. It was fascinating to watch them change and develop, like my own real-life science lessons.

Besides being a teacher, there were two other things I wanted to be when I grew up. From the time I was six, I knew I wanted to be a mother and a hairdresser, too. The mother would obviously have to wait, but the hairdresser I practiced all the time. I had gotten a "life-sized" Barbie head as a gift and I practiced cutting her hair so much, she very quickly ended up bald. I somehow convinced my sister that I had practiced enough and was ready to try cutting her bangs. As you can imagine, it didn't go very well. I definitely got a good scolding and the belt for that one.

Living on the army base meant there were always lots of other families with kids who had also moved around a lot. Army Brats, we were called. Even though when I was at school I was mostly on my own, since apparently no one wanted to be friends with the weird, alien, red-headed kid, I did manage to make a couple of friends on the street where we lived, Billy and Jeanette. Looking back, I think, if those bullies at school had stopped to get to know me, they would have liked Lil' Red and her adventurous, curious, mischievous nature. I was that kid who had all the crazy ideas and wasn't afraid to try them, which of course was

Lil' Red

always fun and exciting until it landed *me* in the emergency room.

There was the time I convinced my good friend Jeanette it was a good idea for both of us to ride in our little red Radio Flyer wagon down our street which was one big hill. The plan was that I would use the handle in the front, turned backward, to steer. Jeanette was my shy, quiet, reserved, opposites-attract kind of friend so it took some serious convincing.

I showed her how we could both easily fit in, if we dangled our legs out over the sides. Then, we both climbed in, I grabbed the handle, and off we went! What could go wrong? The scene that followed would have made the perfect Radio Flyer wagon advertisement!

As we went flying down the hill, screaming at the top of our lungs, my red ponytails wildly waved around. It was all going fine until we got going too fast. My mistake. I'd thought about the steering control, admittedly not a perfect plan, but *not* the fact that we would accelerate as we went — basic physics. I suddenly lost control and swerved right into the back of a parked car. Our neighbor's VW bus. He had been working on the car, so he'd taken off the back bumper. That's right where I ran into the tail pipe with the inside of my left knee. It just popped open, leaving a big gaping hole where I could see all the layers under my skin. So weird. It wasn't even bleeding, it was just a big hole – in my *leg*.

Jeanette immediately freaked out and ran back up the hill to her house. I ran across the street for help, screaming like a banshee and into my house.

My mom was doing something in the kitchen and said, "Oh, Jill. What *now*?" A fair response given my history, I suppose. Imagine her shock at seeing the gaping hole in my

Part One: The Little Wolves

leg. I was definitely off to the ER for stitches—*again*. Since I'd had stitches about once a year since I was one and a half years old, this was nothing new to me by now.

This time, in an effort to distract me from the pain of the numbing shots (injected directly into the wound, very painful) and to keep me calm while they stitched me up, my mom began teaching me multiplication using the dots on the ceiling tiles.

There were other antics, like building a fort in the garage with Billy, that didn't end up in a trip to ER. Actually, it was more of a big shelf, up above the car in the rafters. The framing was already there, so we just had to convince our dads to give us some wood to put down as a floor. From our moms, we needed some sheets to hang up with nails as "walls." We used to hide up there, away from my brother and his friends, sometimes just reading by flashlight or telling ghost stories until we scared each other so much, we ran inside.

One cold, winter day, I decided it would be a good idea for Jeanette and I to "ice skate" down the street. The street itself wasn't frozen, but the water that normally ran down the street gutters was ice, so my idea was for us to just skate along that in our boots. It was fun for a few minutes, until I plowed face first onto the ice. I didn't knock out any teeth, but I did come up with a bloody mouth and killed my right front tooth at the root. Only a few short years later, I would have to endure a root canal at the hands of a notorious army dentist, a traumatic event that would cause a lifelong fear of dentist's offices. Maybe we should have just stuck to regular sledding.

This way of learning by *doing* would continue to be my way throughout my life. I think there are people who *think* about doing things and people who *do* the things. I'm more of a doer. I don't seem to have that filter that stops me, an inner voice that says, "Oh, you could never do *that*." My inner voice is the opposite—it's always cheering me on!

Which is exactly why, on a bright summer day, I decided that Billy and I should build some stilts. I had seen them somewhere and thought, *How hard could it be?* I knew my dad had some wood lying around and figured we'd give it a shot.

We did, in fact, manage to get some footholds nailed to some taller pieces and they ended up putting us about four feet up off the ground. We were only nine years old, so this felt pretty high up for us. It was fun trying to walk around on them in our front yard for a while. That is, until Billy lost his balance and as he tumbled down, he knocked into me and suddenly it was just a pile of wood and bodies.

He was bruised and had sprained his wrist which I got in trouble for, of course—but really, had he not yet learned about the tuck-and-roll kind of falling? And I was mostly just banged up, but with one addition, a small but deep cut above my right eye. It had been a while, so I guess I was overdue... back to the ER for more stitches I went.

Part One: The Little Wolves

Chapter 4

The Fighter

AT SOME POINT, the innocent mischief started to turn more into real trouble. Up until I turned eight, when we moved to Maryland, most of the situations I'd found myself in were of my own doing, me being adventurous, curious and, okay, a little reckless. But then, once I hit third grade things started to shift and became more about me lashing out, fighting back. I mean, I *was* a fiery-tempered redhead, right? I could only take so much before pushing back—literally.

Once, during third grade, I was on the playground at recess when this little blonde, straight-haired girl named Pamela (about as opposite from me as you could be) started making fun of me calling me "Jill the Pill." Seems innocent enough, but it really bugged me since it was something that I heard so often.

And while also excluding me from the game of the day, she was taunting, "No one wants you to play, Jill the Pill," using her meanest sing-song voice.

Something in me just snapped. I turned around and yelled at her to stop. But as I walked away, she spit out one more, "Jill the Pill." That was it! I turned right back around and gave her a big shove.

As she fell, she hit the slide and got a small cut on her leg. She started screaming and wailing like she was dying. *Really?* It didn't even need stitches, I could tell (since I'd already had them a few times by now, I knew). *Clearly* she was not as experienced with these kinds of injuries as I was. Her little drama-queen performance earned me a spot in the principal's office, a place I would also become very familiar with over the next couple of years.

Another day, again out on the playground, a boy named Steven was taunting me, calling me "Banana Butt" (making fun of my good Irish name, Bohannon) *and* "Carrot Top." In this war of words, I had no real ammunition.

I hurled back the standard, "Oh, yeah? Well, you're ugly!" to no effect. He kept dancing around me, singing, "Banana Butt! Banana Butt!" So, I did what any self-respecting ginger would do. I punched him right in the face (with my left fist, of course).

He immediately started crying, and the teacher sent me directly to... you guessed it, the principal's office.

Reflecting on the bullying I experienced led me to contemplate and explore the difference between teasing and bullying. I think the innocent teasing I experienced when I was five and six years old was just that—innocent. It was lighthearted and playful. And when it was obvious I was getting upset by it, it stopped. But as I grew older, the teasing turned to bullying when it was done with malice, with the intention to hurt, shame, and belittle me. And when it was done over and over, relentlessly, day after day.

The bullying didn't stop when I clearly became upset. In fact, that was the reward for the little wolves, and it only

Part One: The Little Wolves

encouraged them to feel stronger and more powerful and to continue the bullying behavior. The taunting was another form of bullying, because it was meant to be cruel and demeaning.

People are generally dismissive when it comes to bullying behavior, waving it off and saying, "Oh, it's just kids being kids" or "All kids are just mean." Kids aren't born bullies. They learn it from adults or from other kids. Maybe they experience abuse at home like I did, and learn that emotional and physical violence is the only way to solve problems. They learn that using force and intimidation gives them a false sense of control over others.

The sad truth is that most child bullies grow up to be adult bullies or abusers. They are at risk for demonstrating aggressive behavior toward their partner and their own children, perpetuating the cycle of violence. This is a cycle we absolutely need to break, and early intervention is key to eradicating domestic violence. We need to shift the culture starting in schools. Fortunately, this movement is well underway in our current society. We're learning more and more all the time and there are numerous organizations advocating against bullying in schools.

I can't tell you why I wasn't one of those kids who turned out to be angry at the world, or why I didn't become just like those little wolves. Maybe, in part, it was because we moved away before the anger took hold of me. I think at the same time I was lashing out and retaliating against the little wolves, I was also drowning in feelings of insecurity and lack of self-worth along with sadness and loneliness. All those feelings were being reinforced at home at the same time, mostly through the abuse from my mother. I was afraid to tell my parents about the bullying at school. I was already in trouble all the time at home anyway, I thought this would be just another thing I was doing wrong. I felt like there was no denying what the world around me was telling me – I was bad. As a result, I became more withdrawn, internalizing my pain. I kept thinking, *maybe I just need to try harder*.

During third and fourth grade I also began to exhibit physical signs of distress from the bullying. I developed a condition where my hands and feet were excessively sweaty, to the point where it caused the skin to constantly peel. They were a sweaty, peeling mess. It was mortifying. And the creams and powders my parents applied to try to fix it only made it worse. It became a sweaty, peeling, *sticky* mess. I didn't wear sandals, only socks and shoes. I kept my hands folded in my lap or tucked in my pockets. It was yet another thing for me to be ashamed of and try to hide away.

I was also having frequent nightmares. All these symptoms were manifestations of my internal suffering, my feelings of loneliness, isolation, and low self-image. The abuse in the form of "discipline," mostly from my mother, my lack of safety, security, and consistent love and affection all fashioned me into a very unhappy, angry Lil' Red, a bit of a volcano ready to blow.

As my anger and frustration increased, so did my outbursts. Most of my trips to the principal's office were for acting out at recess in retaliation against the bullying, but sometimes it was for being disruptive in the classroom. I did very well academically so it wasn't out of frustration with learning. There were many times when one of the boys (usually) would slip me a nasty note or make a mean face, when the teacher wasn't looking. Sometimes they'd even hurl a paper wad or whisper one of their many favorite

Part One: The Little Wolves

mean nicknames. Whenever I would try to retaliate, like throw the paper wad back at them or make faces in response, I always seemed to be the one who got caught. Apparently, I just wasn't devious enough. I did get better at that, though.

Looking back with the lens of a trained teacher after time and experience, I can see that some of my acting out was also due to the fact that I was just bored and uninterested with school. I definitely was not being challenged academically. If you add in pent-up frustration and anger at all of the bullying, at being left out and embarrassed by the teacher, *plus* the abuse I was experiencing at home, with no validation or acknowledgment from anyone, I was bound to explode. No wonder I was lashing out! I was a frustrated, hurt, sad, angry little girl who needed help, guidance, affection, and understanding. But none came.

It didn't help matters at all that, during this time, my brother teased me at home relentlessly, as well. From an outsider's point of view, it must have seemed like just regular sibling rivalry. But I think, because we were so close in age, only eleven months apart—*Irish twins*, as they call it—and because I was already getting teased and bullied at school, my defenses were down and my self-worth and esteem were already low so his meanness packed a lot more punch, figuratively and literally.

My brother invented a punching game where he would punch as hard as he could on my arm and then I would punch him back, until one of us cried *uncle*. I hated that game but I wasn't about to just sit there and get punched, so I punched back. More often than not, before I could win,

I would be the one who got caught and punished by my mother for "picking on" my little brother.

He also called me names and told me I was ugly. His favorite nasty little taunt was, "Pretty is as pretty does, and you're ugly, ugly, ugly!" I think he heard this from Billy's mom. Maybe if this had been the only source of teasing and taunting in my life, I could have withstood it, could have let it roll off and been okay.

But it wasn't, and I couldn't.

I don't know why he and I didn't get along better. We were actually a lot alike. I think he saw me as competition for my parents' attention, especially my dad's. I liked more of the same things as my dad, so I could more easily connect with him, which was harder for my brother. He had his own issues with my dad, being his only son, not living up to his expectations, etc. I'm not sure he ever really worked those out before he died at the young age of forty-nine.

That "life is short" lesson definitely hit home when he died. We all think we have so much time, so we don't prioritize healing and forgiveness. We put it off, because it's emotional and unpleasant, even painful. Cleaning out emotional clutter is hard, it takes some serious work and concentrated effort. Ultimately, we never know how much time we've got, so the time really is now. It's one of those things where there's never really a *good* time. That lesson stuck with me and was something valuable to come from going all the way through the pain of his death and coming out the other side of it with some healing and wisdom.

After our two years in Maryland, we were fortunate enough to be assigned to the beautiful black forests of Munich, Germany. My experience in school there felt

Part One: The Little Wolves

dramatically different. I was now in middle school, for starters, and I attended a combination middle school/high school.

There were a few big differences there, the first being that the culture of this school was probably more worldly than in most middle schools. The kids and teachers there were an eclectic mix, hailing from everywhere around the world. By definition, that created a school culture that was more accepting of differences, because *everybody* was different. There were still cliques and social groups, but even those had a different look and feel from what I had experienced in my previous schools.

The cliques were formed more from practical associations. As an example, the higher-ranking officers' families associated with one another, so those kids naturally bonded. There was the group of stoners and smokers who bonded because they hung out together in the "smoking section" of the school. There were the band kids, the athletes, and other miscellaneous groups formed around common interests. This drew the focus away from physical differences and turned it toward their common ground.

Another difference was that the army base there was a small community, so everyone knew everyone else and it had a tight-knit social structure. Everyone in middle school was busy trying to establish their independence and identity, so any differences between us didn't last for very long. One week, someone might have purple hair and the next week, black. What would be the point in ridiculing someone with red hair? I was still in the less-than-two-percent category, but it just didn't seem to matter as much there.

When we first arrived in Munich, I had a little bit of a hard time fitting in. It was that same old feeling all over again, being the new kid, not knowing anyone, and not knowing which of those social circles I fit into. I wondered again if these kids would accept or reject me. I was at the awkward "tween" age, anyway, with so many physical and emotional changes going on within me that having everything outside also change at the same time seemed a bit overwhelming. I admired how my older sister seemed to take it all in stride, quickly making new friends and identifying with the other athletes. Fitting in at a new school always seemed to come more easily to her.

Although I was greatly relieved to no longer face daily bullying, I still engaged my coping mechanisms, creating a safe, comfortable space for myself in my room at home where I continued to withdraw and spend more time on my own. I also reached out to make at least one good friend who turned out to be my neighbor, Diane. She happened to be exactly my age, and we got along great from day one. All these social differences between the two environments, combined with all the new experiences I had in Munich and the exposure to new cultures, created a new story for me, one that was more about my development and growth than my suffering.

While life outside our family environment was trending in a positive direction, at home it was just the opposite. My mother's absences became more frequent, sometimes she was gone for two or three days at a time. When she *was* around the house, she seemed unhappy and angry. At the time, I felt that anger was directed completely at me.

As I look back on it now as an adult, with the benefit of time and knowledge of events that unfolded over the years,

Part One: The Little Wolves

I can see it was most likely frustration over her deteriorating marriage and her suppressed mental health issues — depression, anxiety and PTSD – that wouldn't fully show themselves until later when we were adults. Her mental health demons were starting to take hold of her when we were children but we were unaware of it at the time. Regardless of the reason, she was not there for me in a supportive, loving way, and continued to use excessive force in her effort to punish, control, and manipulate me.

During our time in the Black Forests of Germany, I was moving forward to find my own identity, forging my strength of character and working toward independence and self-sufficiency. I didn't know it, but I would need all those attributes in the very near future when I found myself living on my own at the age of sixteen. And just as I found my inner strength, my fuck-you gene, to fight back against the little wolves, I would have to draw on that same toughness of spirit again in the near future when I would finally confront my Mama Wolf.

How I wish someone would have told Lil' Red that the bullying wasn't about her, that it was about them, the little wolves. It was about their feelings of inadequacy and self-doubt. It was about them needing to put her down to make themselves feel better. I wish I could go back in time, hug Lil' Red, and whisper in her ear, "It's not you, it's them."

I would tell her to find her voice, to tell them to *stop*. I would tell her if she could ignore them and walk away, it would take away their power and give it to her instead. I would tell her, "You're perfect just as you are, don't change a thing." That all her personality traits are things most people strive for, so she should embrace them, own them. I

Lil' Red

would tell her she is a warrior, strong and fierce. I would tell her she is loved.

And I would absolutely warn her that there are more wolves lurking in the forests of her life.

PART TWO
The Mama and Papa Wolves

*Forgiveness is letting go of the hope
of a different past.*

Lil' Red

Part Two: The Mama and Papa Wolves

Chapter 5

Attachments

I WAS FIVE YEARS OLD when our family piled into our light-green, wood-paneled clad station wagon for the long drive from Washington State to Ft. Hood, Texas, where my dad was stationed. It was glorious. To our delight, we kids were relegated to the way back, where we sat or lay freely, unencumbered and untethered. *Welcome to the seventies.* We were greeted with wide-open spaces, expanses of green grass (*gray-ass*, as I would soon learn to say with a slow, Southern drawl), and thick, hot air heavy with moisture. We quickly settled into our new home, a one-story rambler with a stacked-stone exterior. To an adventurous little redhead with no fear this was a clear invitation to *climb*. None of the neighborhood kids or my siblings would dare, but Lil' Red? She didn't hesitate.

It took me a little while, but I carefully placed each foot and hand as I moved slowly up the wall while my sister, brother, and a few neighborhood kids watched from below holding their breath. Just as I arrived at my intended target at the roofline, my footing slipped and down I went like a sack of potatoes. I landed roughly on my feet before tumbling hard to the ground, crying out in pain.

I think my poor sister thought I might die, the way she went shrieking into the house for help. Once my mother confirmed I wasn't seriously injured and I had only a twisted, swollen ankle to show for my adventure, she scolded me and gave me a lashing to drive her point home: *climbing the side of the house was NOT allowed*. This was the earliest I can remember my mom "spanking" me, although I'm sure it had been going on long before that.

It seemed like it was my mother's mission in life to beat the feisty sense of adventure right out of me. She was determined to make me succumb to her control and become the kind of child who was obedient, dutiful, compliant, and respectful of authority (little did she know, most of those would never be words to describe me at *any* age.)

Whenever I said something that she deemed argumentative or defiant, I got a spanking. When I did or said something "wrong," whenever I caused trouble or "misbehaved" as she perceived it, I got a spanking. When I was little, the frequent spankings were mostly with her hand on my backside, and sometimes with a wooden spoon. Later, it became harsher and more severe, with her using a belt to deliver the blows. I never really understood what it was exactly that I had done to make her so mad. I think it was just me being me.

I've often wondered if her drive to control me was something triggered at my birth, when that doctor announced my arrival saying, "There's trouble." Or maybe it was some stereotype she subscribed to about redheads, maybe a negative association she had from personal experience with someone with red hair, possibly even her own sister. I also wonder if I'd been born a boy whether our relationship would have played out the same way or if her expectations of me would have been different, whether my rambunctious, adventurous, mischievous nature would have been expected rather than rejected.

Although there were changes happening within American culture when I was young, like the Equal Pay Act of 1963 and changes to women's rights, little girls were still expected to be sweet, play quietly with their dolls, help with household chores, and generally be *seen and not heard*, especially those girls from good, conservative Christian homes. I was none of those things. I was a tomboy in every sense. I didn't want to wear dresses, I wanted to wear those Toughskin jeans from Sears like my brother. I wanted to climb, swing, jump and run. Although I will say, my sister and I did enjoy playing with the three-story Barbie house we received for Christmas when I was eight and she was ten... it even came with a convertible car I especially liked, which I'm pretty sure was a Corvette.

My insecure attachment to my mother was likely compounded by the fact that my brother was born just eleven months after me. My mother couldn't possibly have given me the nurturing, affection, and attention I needed when she had another infant to care for. Since my father was either in training or off at war, neither of my parents really met my basic emotional needs—the need to love and be loved, the need to feel safe and a sense of belonging.

When a child is denied those basic needs as I was, it has a huge negative impact on their development. It affected my sense of self-worth, my belief in myself as lovable and capable. It changed how I saw the world. I became less trusting and more skeptical. When adults complimented me on my "beautiful red hair," I was sure they were lying. I was also less affectionate, not wanting to allow others access into my personal space. I didn't trust affection since it conflicted with the anger and abuse I received from my parents, primarily my mom. They were the wolves that I would face daily and live with until sixteen, my mama and papa wolves.

My parents did meet my basic physical needs, however, they fed and clothed me and provided a good home. They made sure I attended school and sent me to church (which in their minds, was just part of a responsible upbringing).

During the year we lived there, I never really acclimated to life in Texas. Life there was different from Washington in pretty much every way. Not only were there big bugs, sticky-hot weather, dangerous spiders, and snakes, but there were also frequent thunderstorms that seemed to always roll through at night.

The loud crashes of thunder between bright lightning strikes absolutely terrified me. Either they would keep me from going to sleep or they'd startle me awake in the middle of the night, at which point I would find my sister and brother and together we would all climb into our parents' bed for asylum.

It wasn't ideal—it was crowded with all five of us—but I took comfort in my position across the bottom of their bed until the storm passed. Eventually, my dad carried me back into my own bed. It took me a long time after that, well into adulthood, to get over my fear of thunderstorms.

I took a little red bus to kindergarten, singing, "The bus, the bus, the B... U... S," while I waited for it. The teacher was nice and the class was fun, but I had already learned basic reading skills and was writing my letters, so I was

Part Two: The Mama and Papa Wolves

generally bored. I used to finish the busy work and then spend the rest of my time playing with toys while I waited for the others to finish. In my report card the teacher noted that I seemed to "hurry" through my work. It was okay though, because it kept me out of my mom's hair and out of trouble. Any escape from my stressful home life was good for me.

Texas is known for its beauty-pageant culture, and I guess my mom couldn't resist entering me into the "Little Miss" contest. Maybe one of the other moms convinced her to do it or she just got a wild hair. I don't remember much about it, just the feeling of awkwardly parading around on stage in my little blue dress. I didn't really care for the whole scene, but I sure liked that big trophy, though! I was relieved when we moved away and I didn't have to do any more of those pageants.

At such a young age, we'd already moved around a few times, and I was developing a distaste for it. So, I was thrilled at the news that we were moving back to Washington, although it ended up being only for a short time. It would mean living near my great-grandparents again which made me happy.

As I described earlier, it was there that I also found a good friend and discovered *cows*. That friendship, and the introduction to farm life and animals, primarily cows, ignited a lifelong love for them. I spent so much time at the farm, helping with chores, caring for the animals, laughing and playing with all the joy that the innocence of childhood brings. I would forever associate cows with those feelings and that place.

That pure joy was overshadowed by my constant feelings of fear. I had learned by then that pretty much everything I did would bring the spankings. Not every day, but they were frequent enough that the punishment felt constant.

I never knew what would set my mother off or spark her anger toward me and this became a source of great stress. I dreaded going home after a day of romping around the neighborhood or playing at the farm, afraid that maybe I'd gotten too dirty, been out too long, done something I shouldn't have, or, God forbid, torn or damaged my clothing in any way.

Truthfully, how I was dressed was such a setup for failure—being forced to wear cute girls' clothes, like dresses and skirts, and then getting in trouble for ruining them. What I *wanted* was to wear were those jeans that came with a guarantee that you'd grow out of them before you ruined them. *That's* what I needed!

The day I fell head over heels off my bicycle, I was more worried about getting in trouble for ruining my bike and my dress than I was about the cut on my elbow and the pain in my arms and legs from the road rash. If I'd had those jeans, I would have had only a fraction of those scrapes and bruises. But my life wasn't about what *I* wanted or who I really was. It was about how the world around me saw me, how my mother expected me to be, forced me to be.

Part Two: The Mama and Papa Wolves

Chapter 6

The Heat of Anger

EVEN AS A CHILD, I knew my Mama Wolf was hitting me out of anger. I could feel the heat of her anger with every blow.

Now, I know there are people out there who don't see anything wrong with this kind of "discipline" and who, for whatever reason, still cling to this archaic, ineffective method for raising a child. Maybe there are even people out there who were abused by a parent in the same ways I was but who weren't affected by it… but I'd guess not many.

For me, especially since I was the main one in my family who received her anger in such a physical way, it had a profound effect. It was excessive and abusive. It wasn't just physical abuse either, it was also verbal and emotional abuse. It was in the way she made me feel by constantly putting me down, punishing me for being me and regularly doling out swift, harsh punishment that was disproportionate to the offense. It was in her constant comparisons of me to my sister, reminding me I wasn't good enough and telling me I should be more like her. It was forcing me to eat food I couldn't stomach and to sit at the table until I did, simply to exert control and punish me for not doing as I was told.

Hitting me didn't teach me self-control, self-discipline, or how to learn from my mistakes. It didn't teach me that I had choices or how to discern right from wrong for myself. What I *did* learn was that hitting was an appropriate response to anger. I learned to be afraid of the person I looked to for comfort and safety, and that making mistakes, being human, and just being me wasn't okay.

The abuse I received as a young girl taught me to comply out of fear rather than a sense of right and wrong. As kids, we're hardwired to seek a connection with trusted adults, especially our mothers, even if that connection feels unstable, unreliable, or unsafe. I learned not to trust, but instead to be skeptical and fearful of those in authority since they were supposed to be the ones protecting me but in reality were the ones who caused pain and trauma. And the biggest lesson of all I learned was that the Mama Wolf always wins, because she's bigger and stronger.

As I grew older, my mother took to using one of my dad's belts as punishment and the spanking evolved, becoming more aggressive and often leaving red marks, bruises, or welts. This was all just a part of normal life for me. It was all I knew growing up.

What I didn't know, and never will, was why I was the main one of us kids to feel the full force of my mother's anger and frustration. I think she was conflicted, not just about her feelings toward me, but about her own life, past and present. There was probably also a strong connection between her conservative religious beliefs and her way of disciplining. Likely, she subscribed to the "spare the rod, spoil the child" theory, believing I would end up becoming

Part Two: The Mama and Papa Wolves

a nightmare child if not handled right. But if that were true, why was it directed more at me than my siblings? Even though I didn't compare notes with them or know all the intimate details of their connection with her, I could see that her expectations, demands, and treatment of me were different.

My siblings and I were all very close in age, my sister was two years older than I and my brother just eleven months younger. My sister was a typical first-born child in many ways. She would have done anything to avoid confrontation, was eager to please, more compliant, and stayed out of my mom's way. She was happy-go-lucky, smart, energetic, athletic, and very social. She did well in school and sports, mostly in track and softball. I think my mom put too much responsibility on her from a very young age to look after my brother and me, which robbed her of some of her childhood innocence. For so many years while we were sharing a bedroom she was my confidant, my close companion, and dearest friend.

My brother was perceived as the "innocent" one, even though he was quite devious himself. He was calmer and quieter than I was, or at least better at hiding his mischievous nature. Ultimately, he was a very sensitive, imaginative, creative soul who tried his best to please our parents, especially my dad, and was just as desperate as the rest of us for our father's time, attention, and approval. As he became a young adult and into adulthood, we discovered my brother's incredible artistic talents from playing multiple instruments to creating incredible art and music.

I did not learn until I was well into adulthood that my brother knew nothing of the heat of our mother's anger which I felt regularly on my backside. This revelation would tragically break our sibling connection for the rest of our lives.

As much as my mother's presence affected me, her absence and inconsistent love did, too. I'm not exactly sure where she was a lot of the time, but her absences from home were frequent and regular. They became even more noticeable when we moved to Maryland.

My mother had taken a part-time job, which accounted for some of her absences, and that meant from the ages of seven, eight, and ten respectively, we were on our own after school. As the oldest, my sister was responsible for my brother and me, which is hard for me to fathom looking back as a parent now myself. I cannot imagine any circumstance when I would feel it appropriate to leave children as young as seven and eight home alone for any length of time, let alone supervised by a ten-year-old. But we didn't know any better back then; it was just life. Like most kids, we just accepted life at face value, without question.

Most days, we walked home from school down the beautiful tree-lined path by our house, made ourselves a snack (my favorite was a bologna sandwich on white bread with mustard), and plopped down on the couch to watch cartoons, play with toys, or run around outside. On one of those afternoons, a sunny spring day just before my ninth birthday, my brother and I were fighting over a toy in the living room.

In our struggle, he pushed me and I fell, hitting my forehead squarely on the sharp corner of the wall by the stairs. (It's worth noting that the responsible ten-year-old was nowhere to be found in that moment.) My forehead

Part Two: The Mama and Papa Wolves

split right open and blood gushed everywhere, which scared my brother so much, he ran and hid.

I held my head and made my way to the bathroom, feeling guilty for bleeding all over everything and knowing full well that somehow, I was going to be the one to get in trouble for this.

As I stood at the bathroom sink, trying to stop the bleeding with a small towel, I thought, *Where is everybody?* I screamed at my brother to go get help. He finally came out from hiding and ran across the street to Billy's house. His mom called our dad.

This time, *he* was the one who took me to the emergency room. We ended up at Walter Reed Hospital, a very large, well-known military hospital where I finally received several stitches after waiting six hours to be seen because I happened to arrive at the same time as a multiple-gunshot victim. They had rolled the wounded woman right by me, covered in blood, screaming and writhing in pain—a memorable event for an eight-year-old.

The nurse apologized for how hard she had to scrub the dried blood off my head because I'd waited so long in the ER. I quietly cried while she cleaned it, with my dad at my side holding my hand. Then came that numbing shot right smack in the middle of the open gash, always the worst part. Even though I'd been through it before and knew what was coming, it was still just as painful. Later that night back at home, as expected my brother was punished for pushing me, but we were both in trouble for fighting and roughhousing. The message wasn't about how there wasn't an adult present to handle the situation, it was about how *we* misbehaved, *we* were wrong.

Lil' Red

Sometimes, my mom was gone for two or three days at a time, but I guess since our dad was with us during those times, it all seemed okay. As we got older, her absences became more frequent. We were never told exactly where she was, but I had the feeling it had to do with the very verbal, heated arguments between her and my dad. Like most things, it was an unspoken rule in our family that this wasn't something we talked about, ever.

When my mother *was* around, she was often engaged in our activities, sewing an outfit or costume for us, volunteering for some event, or arranging outings. These bursts of attention were confusing, since they completely clashed with the anger and hostility that I felt from her, when she was punishing me. I do believe she really was trying in her own way, and doing the best she could.

As is usually the case, there's more to the story than meets the eye. As an adult, I was able to look back at my mother's family history through a less critical, more forgiving lens, and this provided me with the understanding I needed to soften my heart and allow for forgiveness and healing.

My mother, Darlene, was born in Seattle on a crisp autumn day at the end of August, 1942. She was the oldest of six kids. I don't know much about her upbringing except that she came from a deeply troubled family that was burdened with trauma and pain. Hers was more than a checkered past; it was a horrific cocktail of everything from abuse (physical, emotional, and sexual) and mental health issues to financial struggles and questionable life choices on multiple levels.

One of her sisters was a go-go dancer for years (a nice way of saying stripper, back in the day), who lived a party-

Part Two: The Mama and Papa Wolves

girl life of promiscuity, drinking, and drugs. Her other sister suffered from physical abuse by her husband. Later, when she remarried, her second husband sexually abused her daughter and then killed himself out of shame.

Her youngest sister struggled with mental illness and was on disability income and welfare most of her life. She also experienced abuse and was abusive to her two young children, who were taken away from her for a brief time. Her older brother disappeared, and we never knew him or anything about him, only that he must have visited us a few times since he's in a few family photos. And her youngest brother, who was the same age as my sister, struggled with drugs and a reckless lifestyle before getting his electrician's certification and turning his life around.

In her early teens, Darlene had to go live with her grandparents until she graduated high school. There were whispers that the reason was her being sexually abused by her stepfather, but she never outright confirmed that or elaborated on it. In high school, she was the typical beauty queen who got married right after graduation. Apparently, she met my dad shortly after, and they were so taken with each other, they both left their respective spouses and married each other when she was just twenty, welcoming my sister to the world not too long after.

When I came along two years later and then my brother soon after that, we were "three under three," which would be overwhelming for any young mother. Then, my father entered the military and was gone often for weeks at a time. He even went to war in Vietnam for nearly a year, which had to have been completely overwhelming and stressful for my mother. Since we rarely lived near extended family, she didn't have much of a support system either.

Lil' Red

Looking back, it does seem like my mother saw an opportunity to create a better life for herself with my dad, and she did her best to make that a reality. Even if she did marginally better than the life she'd known growing up, it would be a huge accomplishment. The ghosts of her painful past and genetic family history of mental illness and trauma would eventually win in the end, but it didn't stop her from trying. My father's absences ultimately had a long-lasting impact on everyone in our family, not just Darlene.

Part Two: The Mama and Papa Wolves

Chapter 7

Absent Papa Wolf

TO THE OUTSIDE WORLD, our family was picture-perfect, idyllic. The handsome, athletic, decorated military officer and war veteran with his beauty-queen wife by his side and three beautiful well-dressed children who were all smiles. They say a picture is worth a thousand words, but our annual family photos from Olan Mills or Sears didn't tell the whole story. Behind the curtain of appearances was a disjointed, disconnected, fractured family that was slowly unraveling.

At the helm of our sinking ship was my dad, Roger, or "Raj" as his friends called him. He was born in northern Minnesota, in Bemidji, back in 1938 to an extremely conservative minister and his wife. He grew up in a strict, Christian home, meat-and-potatoes all the way. I don't know much about him as a child, but at his funeral, I learned from his sisters that, as a boy, he loved catching frogs just like I did, except *he* was fond of carrying them around in his pockets!

His striking good looks developed at a young age: he had a full head of wavy, light-brown hair with hints of red, blue eyes, and a flashy smile. Roger had a big presence and a big smile to match. When he entered the room, everyone took notice. When he spoke, people listened. He had an electric energy that was engaging and contagious. He was eloquent, confident, and well-spoken with a velvety bass voice. That *voice*. One of my very favorite memories from childhood was on Sundays, when he sang his solos in the choir. It was so moving, it brought tears to my eyes every time.

To me, he was bigger than life, and not only physically. He'd been a football player and maintained his fitness out of necessity for the military, but he also represented strength, power, comfort, and security. Especially when he was in uniform. He was a crucial but elusive piece to the puzzle of my need for love and affection.

As an officer in the military, his job required him to be away from home often, sometimes for great lengths of time. He served in Vietnam for a year when I was just two, and he often spent weeks at a time out on "maneuvers," which were exercises where a unit would simulate combat scenarios in a field setting. As an officer, he played a critical role in those exercises. I always felt like this was one part of his job that he thoroughly enjoyed. As kids, we didn't understand the importance of his job or appreciate the sacrifices he made for our country. We just knew it meant he wasn't home with us a lot of the time.

When he *was* home, he was usually engaged in one of his many hobbies—either home repairs, fixing or building things, fishing, camping, hunting, or just about anything having to do with cars. Sometimes, to our great delight, he would engage with us in a wrestling match or tickle fight, sledding, skiing, or playing a sport. These were the times when I remember him freely showing emotion.

I did overhear countless arguments between my parents, and I felt worried by how angry they both sounded, as they were often yelling at each other. When I was in my teens, in my "black sheep" rebellious phase, he was definitely angry with me many times, although he didn't raise his voice or hand to me.

I think another reason he withheld his emotions was probably partially due to the fact he was *trained* to not show emotion. His success as an officer and soldier depended on it. It was also the norm for men in his generation to hold in their emotions and to remain stoic at all times, in order to portray the strong, masculine persona that commanded respect and authority. It was a common belief in the sixties that a father's job was to provide for his family financially and maintain a firm disciplinary style, something that was reinforced in his conservative upbringing and then his army training. It was normal for the father to be the provider while the mother was expected to be the nurturer. My guess is he was emotionally spent after battling his war demons, fighting with my mother, and rising to the challenge of his physically and mentally demanding job. The fact that he was able to muster any kind of joy, enough to share with us, was kind of a miracle, considering what he must have been through.

My father was a good provider. We always had a solid roof over our heads, food on the table, nice clothes, new toys on birthdays and Christmas, and access to whatever extracurricular activities and sports we wanted to pursue. He always got super-excited about our sports, whether it was coaching my sister's and my softball teams or my

Lil' Red

brother's Little League baseball team or being the loudest person cheering for my sister at her track meets. He did play the role of disciplinarian in our family as well, enforcing the strict household rules laid down by he and my mother and occasionally doling out the physical punishment.

The one thing we desperately lacked from our father was time and attention. With the three of us vying for his attention, I learned at a pretty young age that the best way to get my share of it was to be interested in the things he enjoyed. That's how I found myself, at age ten, sitting in a small fishing boat at 5:00 in the morning, quietly waiting for a tug on the line that never came and at age twelve, learning how to gut a deer. I hated getting up so early, I hated being cold and having to sit still and be quiet for so long, and I hated the stinky, messy fish and the idea of shooting an animal. But I loved being with my dad, so I went – hunting, fishing, camping, all of it.

Like him, I loved being out in nature, so I tagged along on his camping and hunting trips whenever he let me. Being outdoors with him was like having my own personal Boy-Scout survival training. As an expert due to his military experience, my dad taught me all the basic outdoor skills, from setting up camp to making a fire. He even coached me on how to cook and eat rattlesnake, although I never had the chance.

My favorite time was cooking over the campfire and then sitting around, telling stories, or just looking at the stars. I still love sitting and talking by a fire to this day. His stories were never personal, though. They were always more centered around us kids, extended family, or learning about the outdoors. It always felt like he wanted to connect with us, but only on a certain level, never to the point of letting his guard down or sharing anything too personal.

When I turned eleven, he insisted that, if I was going to be around his guns, I needed to get my National Rifle Association certification, a reasonable and responsible request. I signed up and attended classes one night a week, trying to ignore the fact that I was the only girl there.

I had nearly completed the course and was doing well until the final chapter, when I had to watch a long, detailed video on how to gut and clean a deer. In a group of about twenty students, I was the only one crying as we watched that video. I didn't care. It was just too much for me. I did see it through and got my certification in the end, grateful I didn't have to *prove* my deer gutting skills. Afterward, I adamantly proclaimed I would never actually shoot a "poor animal" and didn't do much hunting after that. I was still damn proud of myself though, for seeing it through and getting that license.

There were other hobbies of his I took interest in that stuck, and some even became lifelong passions and interests that led to other pursuits. From a young age, maybe six or seven, I loved helping my dad when he was fixing things, anything from cars to house projects and everything in between. It started out as something I would do to be closer to him, but the more I learned about all the different tools and how to use them, the more I loved it.

I loved the smell of the wood, the challenge of figuring out how to build something, and the satisfaction of a completed project. As an adult, I became the "fixer" in my household, always engaged in some kind of do-it-yourself project. I even started a group with my girlfriends and called it The Project Club, where a few of us met up once a month and spent a day doing projects on our "honey-do" lists. It was brilliant. I taught my friends how to use tools and do a lot of basic repairs or projects, and by joining forces and setting aside focused time out of our busy lives, we all learned new skills while getting things done—and had a great time together doing it!

Another passion of my dad's that profoundly influenced me was his interest in cars. When we were younger, the cars we had were all very practical and primarily for the purpose of transporting our big family of five. When I was five, we had a light-green station wagon with wood paneling, and we loved riding in the way back of it for long trips. We also had a couple of different Buick sedans that we glided around in, and we even took one with us to Europe while we lived there (which was a huge mistake on those twisting, narrow roads).

My father did manage to acquire a few good toys throughout the years. One summer, we had a speed boat, we also had a large Airstream camper for a short time, and he even had a motorcycle when I was nine. Interesting fact, that motorcycle purchase was right around the time he was in his mid-thirties.

My clearest memory of that motorcycle was of him riding away on it with his bags strapped to the back, while I stood, crying and waving, as he drove away. Even though I didn't fully know what was happening, I knew it was something significant and it wasn't good. I think he and my mother actually separated for a little while. You'd think I would've hated motorcycles after that traumatic moment, but I actually loved them as an adult and eventually got my motorcycle license. I enjoyed riding for a few years, although, ultimately, I pursued other hobbies.

Part Two: The Mama and Papa Wolves

The seed of passion for all things cars was planted, and as I got older, once I turned eighteen, I was fully obsessed. My dad taught me to drive at sixteen, mostly because I was a more "aggressive" driver than my mother was comfortable with, and after an intense driving session that ended with her digging her fingernails into the dash, she refused to ride with me. He taught me on his old manual Datsun B210, which I enjoyed so much more than that big, floaty boat of a Buick, anyway. Much later in life, once I was in my mid-forties, I finally converted my lifelong interest in cars into a hobby and obtained my amateur racing license. I think my dad, Raj, would have loved that. I don't race anymore, but I've owned some amazing sports cars and still get immense joy from driving.

I learned so much from him, and not just the obvious like how to use tools, my interest in cars, or the camping and survival skills, but also about strength of character, standing up for what you believe in, loyalty, and determination. I learned from him that if you believe you can do something, nothing can stop you. I wish I could have had more time with him, to know him as an adult and to learn more about his life, his childhood, and experiences at war. I only knew him as my elusive, larger-than-life father who made forgivable mistakes and failed as my protector, my papa wolf.

Chapter 8

Forgiveness

OUR MOVE TO MARYLAND when I was eight meant being far away from our relatives in Washington and Idaho. About as far away as we could be, in fact, without leaving the country (that would come soon, but we didn't know it yet). Although the bullying from the little wolves at school grew much worse there, I still managed to find things I enjoyed.

Along with exploring the woods, catching frogs, riding my bike and occasionally playing with friends, I also started gymnastics class a couple of days a week after school. The thing I really enjoyed about gymnastics was that it was an individual sport, so I didn't have to wait to be chosen for a team or partner with anyone or even try to make friends there. It was an escape from the bullying, and I could just go there and do the thing I enjoyed. It turned out I was pretty good at it, too, and would continue pursuing gymnastics for the next few years until I hurt myself and decided to stop.

Not long after I began gymnastics class, I had to take a break for a couple of months after the wagon *incident* and

Part Two: The Mama and Papa Wolves

stitches, the healing of which was prolonged by their premature removal. The day I'd gotten my stitches out, I was helping my brother set the table for dinner. We were goofing around as usual, running back and forth from the kitchen to the table, when I tripped on the edge of the carpet and landed square on my knee. *Pop!*

I looked down at my incision, which was now bleeding profusely, and was immediately beside myself with anguish, knowing full well it meant another trip to the ER, another shot right in the center of the wound, and of course, another round of stitches. My mom was right there for that one, so she ended up staying with me while they stitched me up. She gave me another lesson in multiplication to distract me. I just had to learn things *the hard way*.

A year later, in that same living room, I had one of my most memorable birthdays. One thing my mother did consistently was to make our birthdays special. We usually had friends over for cake and a small party. Occasionally, one of our birthdays aligned with a visit to extended family, and then we'd have a bigger celebration.

On my tenth birthday, she went all out. She organized a fifties "sock hop"-themed party with a few of my friends. We all dressed in poodle skirts, white shirts, and saddle shoes, with our hair in high ponytails. It was the absolute most fun! I loved how she danced with us in the living room, teaching us how to jitterbug and boogie-woogie. When I blew out my candles, my wish was for life to be like that all the time. I wanted the fun-loving, engaging mom to stick around.

But fun mom never stuck around for long. Being a good caregiver and a good mother aren't the same thing. She couldn't do both, and her mixed messages were really starting to take a toll on me. On the one hand, she did things that a caring and attentive mother would do, like activities with me and birthday parties and sewing clothes for me and my sister. She also sent the constant message that I was bad, that nothing I did was right, that I was the black sheep of the family. And the more she told me that's what I was, the more I believed it and became it. A sort of self-fulfilling prophecy.

Another of her mixed messages was served up with dinner. My mother provided our basic meat-and-potatoes meals with some regularity. She forced me to eat foods I didn't like and that actually made me gag, mostly canned carrots and peas, and the occasional salad of iceberg lettuce with mealy tomatoes and Italian dressing. I would have gladly eaten bowls full of spinach, broccoli, corn, cauliflower, and even brussels sprouts, but instead she forced me to eat the few things I couldn't stomach. She also forced me to drink milk. I hated milk. Much, much later, once I was an adult, I confirmed I'm genetically lactose intolerant, but she couldn't have known that then. Back then, it was considered a staple of a healthy diet, and I was forced to choke it down with every meal.

This power play always ended up with me in tears, forced to sit at the table alone long after dinner was over and often until bedtime, until I ate the now ice-cold food. I wasn't a picky eater, I ate most things, but there were a few I just couldn't eat and still can't to this day. But she was hellbent on making her point that she was the one in control and that I had to do what she said, without question, or else. So, I learned to fake-chew my food and swallow it whole with milk. Sometimes, I excused myself to the bathroom with a mouthful and spit it all out in the toilet.

Again, it was the same message that she was the one in control, it was her way or no way, and my only choice was to yield to it—or else. It's only been just in the last ten years that I have finally learned to sit and eat by myself without feeling anxious and uncomfortable. It's still not my preference, but I can do it. I even make it a point to take time to cook a full meal for myself, something appetizing and healthy, honoring the choice to nourish my body with food I like and enjoy eating.

The constant battles over food and behavior followed by abuse began to take their toll, with my inner suffering showing itself outwardly. With each passing day, I grew angrier and more withdrawn, especially at school, along with becoming more anxious and defensive. As I described earlier, I even developed physical symptoms of my anxiety and stress in the form of excessively sweaty hands and feet to the point that they were an embarrassing, peeling, sweaty mess.

As the bullying escalated at school, so did my retaliation. All the anger I was experiencing at home was unconsciously turned right around and thrown back at the bullies at school. When I got in trouble for lashing out against them, those in authority would tell me that hitting others was wrong. But since it's what my mom did to me and it was what I knew, I found it all very confusing.

And no one told me what to do with all my rage. They didn't offer any alternatives, so what was I supposed to do? It was the same message repeated—that I was wrong, my behavior was wrong, and my feelings were all wrong. There was no validation, no understanding, no sympathy, and no help.

Lil' Red

We weren't aware of it as kids, but our mother suffered from some undiagnosed mental illnesses: depression, PTSD, and anxiety disorder. To us, our mom was just our mom. We didn't compare notes with other kids we knew or exchange information on how their moms were the same or different. Truthfully, we never lived anywhere long enough to get close with other families and have those kinds of in-depth comparisons. From a kid's perspective, all parents are kind of weird anyway, right? We accept most adults and authority figures at face value, at least until we get older, when we have more experience and a more critical eye.

Later, when my siblings and I were adults and our mom was in her early fifties, her battle with the mental health demons finally consumed her. She had remarried a few years after divorcing my father when I was eighteen, and soon after her new husband died, unexpectedly and tragically, in a boating accident. This traumatic event led her to develop an addiction to prescription drugs that has plagued her for the rest of her life and robbed her of her vitality and mental and physical health.

His death sent her into an emotional spiral that brought all her mental health issues to the forefront. It was as if the thread holding her together had snapped, and the demons she had kept hidden away for so many years finally came into the light. Once we saw them out in full view, it was easy to look back on our childhood experiences, situations, and her behavior and attribute them to her struggle with those conditions.

Just a couple of years later, my father also passed away at the young age of fifty-nine from Colon Cancer. I spent the year and a half after his diagnosis and leading up to his

Part Two: The Mama and Papa Wolves

death visiting with him in Arizona when I could, often with my three young daughters in tow.

I'd decided to reconcile and forgive him for what I perceived as his transgressions against me—moving to an apartment when I was sixteen with no room for me and forcing me out of the house, abandoning me in my time of excruciating pain and suffering, and disclosing my location to my abuser, putting me in danger and causing me to have to flee again. My father also had no communication with me for several years after that, not until I had my first child, at which point we slowly started to rebuild our relationship.

I knew my father's days were numbered, so I decided not to pursue a full reckoning on all my grievances. He was in enough pain already. We did have a few discussions about how things could have been different between us, and he acknowledged he hadn't been as supportive as he'd have liked.

He expressed that he wished he'd stayed in contact with me after I got married. By way of explanation, he shared about how he had struggled with his new marriage for years and that had consumed his time and attention.

Once we found a place of resolution, we moved on to reminiscing about the past. We spent our time together looking at old photos, retelling stories, and remembering good moments. That in and of itself was also incredibly healing—to focus on all the good, rather than just the bad.

When my dad finally passed, it was excruciatingly painful for me. We honored his years of military service with the flag presentation and gun salute, but I couldn't tear myself away from his coffin. I wasn't ready to let him go. Just like in childhood, I needed more time.

Chapter 9

A New School Culture

THE NEXT PORT FOR MY shipwreck of a family was the Black Forests of Munich, Germany. We were all excited about this move, as we'd never been out of the country (other than my dad, of course). I had no real expectations, but I hoped I'd be able to see some of the places I'd learned about in school, like the castles in Germany (Neuschwanstein in particular, the "Disney" castle), the Eiffel Tower, the Louvre, and the Swiss Alps.

As it turned out, while my father was assigned in Munich, one of the greatest gifts our parents gave us was extensive travel, so I did get to experience all of those places and more. I'm forever grateful to them for planting the seed that grew into a lifelong passion for travel, adventuring, and exploring new places and cultures.

While we lived there, I also found some relief from the bullying, although I still had a hard time fitting in. Because there were more diverse cliques in middle school than in elementary, I was able to find safe harbor with the misfits and stoners.

Part Two: The Mama and Papa Wolves

As I mentioned, in Munich, we attended a unique school there, a combined middle and high school for army "brats," which turned out to be a pretty great place to serve my middle school "sentence" (after all, that's what middle school feels like, doesn't it?). We had an eclectic mix of teachers and students from all walks of life. I went there at a time when I was open to the influences and experiences that came my way.

The teachers at MAHS (Munich American High School) were not your ordinary teachers. I'm not sure where they all came from, exactly, or why they were there, but most of them were American civilians (non-military). Regardless of why they were there, you could tell they were at MAHS because they were passionate about teaching. They were there by *choice*, no one was forcing them to work there.

One of the teachers, Mr. Butler, was a strong-featured African American man, probably in his early forties, who taught history with a great sense of humor, animation, and a lighthearted approach. He managed to make learning about history fun and engaging. He had a way of making it come alive and feel current and relevant. Then there was Mr. Henderson, the older, graying English teacher, who presented himself as a rough hardass who signed our papers with his self-appointed nickname, *The Monster*. Underneath this facade, it was clear that he cared a great deal about each of his students and was passionate about all things English.

He made us memorize Shakespeare, write long essays, and read books we didn't want to read—he pushed us, and we rose to meet his expectations. One of my favorite assignments, one I never forgot, was his prompt, "A Little Knowledge is a Dangerous Thing." He told us to write a two-page essay about what that meant to us. I respected the way he made us think *outside the box*.

There was Mr. Morrison, the long-haired hippie band teacher who brought his mop of a dog to class every day. He had an easy way of teaching music that made you want to be better and do better, just for the joy of it.

Mrs. Donaldson taught home economics. Bless her heart—she was old and wrinkled with thinning hair that she colored a dark black and tried desperately to tease, to make it look fuller than it was. She was only mildly interested in the subjects she was supposed to teach as part of the course: basic cooking, sewing, and anything else she felt young girls needed to know to become good homemakers. Mostly, she just gave us whatever instructions for the task that day and then sat at her desk, messily applying bright-orange lipstick with shaky hands or whatever other distraction she could muster, sometimes even taking a little nap, while we got busy being up to no good.

One of my stoner friends from shop class, Kiki, had the foresight to bring weed butter with her on the day we were making brownies. Our team of four didn't waste any time whipping up our special brownies. Mrs. Donaldson didn't even notice. She was just glad when class was over and we hadn't set the school on fire. I did manage to complete my sewing project, a T-shirt that I proudly wore for years. I was pretty proud of the fact that it lasted long enough for me to outgrow it *before* it fell apart.

There wasn't a class I didn't like, but shop class was definitely my favorite because I got to use all the tools that I had learned to love through helping my dad. And, truth be told, I didn't mind that it was full of mostly boys. I found

Part Two: The Mama and Papa Wolves

I connected easily with the few girls in that class, as most of them were tomboys like I was.

The kids in that class were mostly stoners or punks, set apart from the general population by their lifestyle choices, clothing, and behavior. They didn't dress like the other kids and didn't talk like them, think like them, or act like them. This appealed to me, along with the fact that, because they were such an eclectic bunch who believed in self-expression and individualism, they readily accepted newcomers and those who were also outcasts, even if for different reasons.

My red hair was a non-issue. They could have cared less. They didn't impose their choices on me, didn't require me to smoke or sneak sips of cheap vodka from their flasks out back of the shop like they did, and they didn't care how I looked or dressed. They just accepted me for me. This was a new experience for me.

All my teachers, other than maybe old Mrs. Donaldson, were engaging, challenging, and inspiring. Finally, a school experience where the focus was on the learning and the growing, and not the bullying or how I didn't fit in. My exposure to this kind of impassioned, creative, inventive way of teaching would inspire me to become a teacher. Even though I only ended up teaching part-time, other than the one year when I managed and taught my own preschool, I always tried to emulate the genuine creativity I had experienced from these teachers as a student.

This school's culture was heavy on sports. My sister was on the track team and was in the popular crowd. Naturally, I was a little cooler just by association, all her friends knew me as Kellie's little sister. Everyone attended track meets, football games, basketball and volleyball games religiously. There were pep rallies on the night before big games, too.

And school rituals, like the seniors repainting the elephant statue in front of the school at the end of each year.

There were the usual after-school clubs, and the one that appealed to me most was the yearbook club. I really only joined because my friend, Mikki was in it, but I soon realized I enjoyed taking photos, writing articles, and helping with the assembly and production.

Because MAHS was such a small, close-knit community, where everyone knew everyone, the tragedy that struck during our second year there hit very hard. A group of kids, ages fifteen to eighteen, were crossing the street when a drunk driver in a van careened into them killing several, including a couple of my sister's close friends.

This tragedy brought our little community to its knees. I had no idea how to console my sister and couldn't relate to her pain. All I could really do was stay out of her way and let her mourn alongside her friends.

I made fast friends with my neighbor, Diane, who was also in band class with me. She and I were in the same grade. She played the flute, and I played the clarinet—okay, *played* is a bit of a stretch. I was trying to *learn* to play the clarinet, and it wasn't going well.

I really wanted to learn the drums but that was taken, and there was no way to practice it at home anyway. Diane had gotten braces and was fully in the throes of her awkward "tween" phase, shy and low on self-esteem like I was. We were a perfect fit.

There were the usual adolescent growing pains of middle school, like teasing and awkwardness plus separations between social groups, but generally speaking, school life was significantly better for me while I was at MAHS. Unfortunately, home life did not follow suit.

Part Two: The Mama and Papa Wolves

Chapter 10

Broadening Horizons

OUR HOME IN MUNICH was simple but nice enough. It was an older two-story duplex on a street that was the dividing line between the army base housing and the German community. There were no fences, no signs, and nothing restricting movement between the two areas. It was just right there. There was an unspoken rule, however, that we didn't cross that imaginary line, although I never knew the specific reasons why.

One block over was the S-Bahn train station, and behind our house was a dirt path lined with a variety of big trees, and that's how we walked to and from school each day. I loved walking that path, with the sunlight peeking through the trees, casting shadows, the wind rustling the leaves, and the crunch of sticks, rocks, and pinecones under my feet.

This was the first house we lived in where I didn't share a room with my sister. It took me a while to adjust, but with the help of my mother, who reluctantly agreed to find me a lime-green rug and some cow posters, I made it my own. When I wasn't playing with Diane, I was mostly alone. My sister had a large group of friends and either hung out with them or was running track. We both played softball but on different teams. My brother had his own friends, but I think he spent a lot of time on his own, too. My dad was gone often, as usual, and my mother became more absent than ever. My mom was around enough to continue to exert control over me, she seemed more desperate than ever. And the physical abuse, mostly with a belt, continued as well.

One crisp, fall day, as the brightly colored leaves rustled in the wind, I raced home from school with my sweatshirt tied tightly around my waist. It was there to cover up the big stain on my pants where I'd bled through them. I'd gotten my first period while in shop class, which, luckily for me, was my last class of the day, so I'd just excused myself to the bathroom and didn't go back.

I honestly had no idea what was happening. I went to my room when I got home and cried, not knowing what to do. No one was home for me to ask. No one had bothered to tell me what to expect. Diane was the only person who noticed I'd left school early when I wasn't at the elephant statue out front after school, which was our meeting spot to walk home together. As soon as she arrived at my house, she knocked on our front door to check on me. When I peeked out of my bedroom window and saw it was her, I ran down to let her in.

I hurriedly explained to her what had happened, and since she'd already gotten her period a few months before, she reassured me then ran next door to her house to get me some of her supplies. She kindly showed me what to do and that was that.

There was never any explanation or reassurances from my mother. No apology or attempt to assist after-the-fact, when she found out what had transpired. I was actually

Part Two: The Mama and Papa Wolves

worried that I would be in trouble for staining my pants. It was just something I had to figure out for myself, like so many other things. All the confusing thoughts and feelings of adolescence, all the life changes that came with moving to another country, and all of the new experiences and adventures in this new land were *all* up to me to figure out. Fortunately, I did have a couple of close friends, like Diane, with whom I could share my thoughts, feelings, and worries. That lesson, the difference that a good, trusted friend can make in your life, was one that would stick with me forever.

I also had friends I looked to, not for sharing confidences, giving support, or expressing secrets, but for more adventurous pursuits. These were the friends I'd made in shop class, the smokers and stoners. They were used to defying authority and making their own choices. It was with one of those friends that I figured out how to hop the train to downtown Munich.

Just before my brother died at the age of forty-nine, he and I compared notes about life in Munich and discovered we were both, separately and unbeknownst to the other, doing the exact same thing—hopping the train with friends to go down to Munich city center.

When I went with my friends, we would either get some of our favorite foods (sausage, schnitzel, pretzels) and, if funds and opportunity allowed, beer, or we'd just walk around or sit in one of the squares, people-watching. It was fairly innocent mischief, nothing malicious or illegal, just us stretching our adolescent legs a bit.

It was surprisingly easy. Our parents had no idea, of course, and we never would have been allowed but things were different in Europe. The Europeans had different views on pretty much everything, from kids having a bit of wine or beer to how restricted or freely they were allowed to interact with the outside world.

Since I'd been hanging out with the stoners and smokers, I was curious to try smoking, so I saved up my allowance and planned to buy a pack of cigarettes. It involved me daring to cross that imaginary border on the next block.

I took my time, casually walking through their neighborhood, since I was also curious about the differences in their lives. I discovered they had cigarette machines on the corners here and there. I found a secluded spot over at the park behind our house, where I went occasionally to sit, ponder life, and smoke my cigs. I found it relaxing and kind of meditative.

Fortunately, it was a short-lived habit, limited to my time in Munich, as it was more about accessibility and the influence of the kids I spent time with there. But the lesson I learned about connecting with nature as a source for inspiration, relaxation, and introspection would stick with me.

After that, I started strolling through the streets of the German community regularly, just observing people as I went. Between my periodic trips to the town center and my wandering around the neighborhoods, I felt like I was fully immersed in German culture. We also had German lessons at school, and I quickly became nearly fluent, communicating easily with the few German friends I had from church.

Besides my secret explorations, I also engaged in many cultural activities that *were* condoned by my parents. I participated in the handbell choir through our church,

Part Two: The Mama and Papa Wolves

where I even had to wear a dirndl dress for our performances. I was given permission to join in on ski trips with a group of kids from church. My parents reasoned that it was a group of individuals with higher morals and standards of behavior, so it would be "safe" for me to join them. Truth was, they were just as mischievous, deviant, and degenerate as any other kids, maybe more so, because they'd mastered the art of deceit and could appear innocent while secretly misbehaving.

On one occasion with the innocent deviants when I was thirteen, I was fortunate to have the opportunity to learn to ski in Austria. I was with a group of about thirty kids, accompanied by a few adult chaperones, and we stayed in an old castle. We didn't care that it was cold, dark and damp. It was an *actual* castle. We certainly didn't learn much about God or the Bible on that trip, but we definitely had a good time. There was the usual innocent fun, like sneaking out after curfew for snowball fights or to drink a beer or two, lots of flirting and teasing, and some making out. All normal parts of growing, changing adolescent behavior.

For a couple of seasons, I played on a softball team that traveled by bus throughout southern Germany, Sud Bayern, for our games and tournaments. This wasn't much different than school groups going on field trips, but it was outside of school and something we did without much supervision.

Surprisingly, my parents even let my sister travel back to the U.S. on her own on a flight from Munich to Estes Park, Colorado, when she was just fifteen for a teens' church retreat. It seemed we'd found our loophole. Normally, our parents were extremely conservative and strict in all things. But while we were living in Germany, they seemed to loosen the reins and started to allow more freedom and independence, adopting more of the European way of life. The "when in Rome," in our case Munich, attitude. Or maybe they were just too absorbed in their own lives, their declining marriage, or who knows what else, to take notice or care.

I was excited to discover a new world of food outside of the despised canned peas and carrots while in Germany—sausage, brats, spaetzle, schnitzel, sauerbraten, sauerkraut, and Nutella on toast. I loved it all. I absorbed every bit of German culture I could, from learning to speak German to experiencing Oktoberfest (we had to sneak into a tent), the famous Glockenspiel, and the Munchner Chriskindlmarkt (Christmas Market). I adored the Zimmerfreis (bed and breakfasts) with their doubled-up, fluffy down duvets. I would forever be ruined and spoiled by those incredibly comfortable beds, a feeling I've strived to recreate in every one of my homes since. And, of course, the endless castles, forests, rivers, and mountains. I fell in love with every bit of it.

The combination of all these new, liberating experiences, from meeting new people, friends, and teachers to discovering new ways of looking at the world, along with the exposure to a new culture, transformed me. I discovered the taste of independence, self-reliance, and self-sufficiency, and there was no going back. When we left Germany to return to Washington at the age of fourteen, I couldn't have known how all these factors and influences would come together to transform my life so definitively, but I had a great awakening and huge shifts waiting for me there.

Part Two: The Mama and Papa Wolves

While I was enjoying my rich adolescent awakening, my mother seemed to be mired down even more deeply in her own anger and misery—anger with herself, her life with my dad, and with me. Although she didn't have direct knowledge of most of the mischief I was up to, she still managed to find plenty wrong with my behavior, which again warranted her violent form of punishment. Whether I accidentally broke something of hers, was talking back (meaning I disagreed with her), had lost my jacket, or if she caught me swearing, the punishment was the same. It was less frequent, mostly because I just wasn't around home as much, but it still happened.

I was learning to bury my anger and keep my feelings to myself. Also, I started to avoid being at home. Between my sports, the occasional trips downtown, extracurricular activities, overnights with the church groups, and general hanging out with friends, it wasn't hard to spend most of my time away from home. Since my dad was gone so much with work and my mom was wherever she was (we didn't know), there wasn't much family togetherness.

Around this time, I also started cooking family meals. I was enjoying learning to cook in my Home Ec class at school, and since our mother's presence was inconsistent, I just pitched in and made a couple of meals each week. Friday nights I made pizza. Occasionally, on another night, I made something simple, like a meatloaf or a casserole. I liked cooking, and it felt like a meaningful way of contributing. This was the start of my lifelong interest and passion for cooking at home.

One of the smartest things my parents did while we were stationed in Germany was to travel around Europe with us as a family. They took a couple of trips on their own, as well, but we took several trips as a family. We were limited to places we could drive to in our big boat of an American car, the long, heavy, dark-green, gas-guzzling 1975 Buick LTD we'd brought with us. That car embodied everything American. We must have looked so ridiculous, cruising around Europe in that car. There were so many narrow, cobbled streets that we could *not* fit through, but somehow my dad managed to make his way throughout Germany, Austria, and France.

Those travels, along with my exposure to new cultures, food, and ways of life, sparked my life-long passion for exploring the world. Living in Germany for a couple of years during such a critical stage in my development would prove to be pivotal in my growth and maturation as a human and individual. And, as I would soon find out, it would lead to a climactic turning point in my relationship with my mom.

Honestly, if I could have stayed in Germany when my family moved back to Washington State, maybe as an exchange student or with another family, I absolutely would have.

Part Two: The Mama and Papa Wolves

Chapter 11

Finding My Voice

OUR FAMILY RECENTLY HAD relocated back to the U.S., back to Washington, the Evergreen State, to a suburb of Seattle, in Tacoma. I was fourteen years old, just finishing my freshman year of high school.

On another typical gloomy, gray, rainy spring day in the Northwest, my new friend, Benita, and I had missed the bus, so we decided to make the best of the mile-long walk home in the pouring rain. We splashed recklessly in puddles, singing and laughing as though we didn't have a care in the world.

I didn't give any thought to the fact that all that water would be bad for my leather loafers, but, of course, they were ruined by the time I got home. I happily skipped through the front door and kicked them off before heading to the kitchen for a snack. When my mother saw them, she was livid. She yelled at me, calling me irresponsible and disrespectful, and saying I had no appreciation for the nice things she and my dad worked so hard to provide for me. She accused me of just throwing it back in their faces.

Lil' Red

She had turned what seemed like an innocent and joyful day for me into a deliberately destructive act of aggression toward her personally. She went one step further and followed me into my room, belt in hand, prepared to deliver what she deemed the necessary and appropriate punishment.

She took one swing with the belt, which landed squarely on the back of my upper leg and immediately made a huge, red welt. I turned around and grabbed the belt before she could hit me again. Then, I looked her in the eye and said, "Never again."

This was the moment I decided I had had enough of her abuse. I don't know why that day was different for me than any other day, maybe it was my "fuck-you gene" finally kicking in. Some call it resiliency, or determination, but whatever you call it, I had reached my breaking point and realized she no longer had power over me. I could understand and even agree with dishing out appropriate, non-violent punishment—maybe force me to use my allowance to buy new shoes or lose a privilege. But I didn't deserve this beating, and I knew it. That was the last time my mother laid a hand (or a belt) on me. We didn't talk about it again until fifteen years later.

That day sparked a change in me. It was a catalyst for my realization that I had a voice, my own voice, my own thoughts. One of the many things I became more vocal about after that was my internal conflict with my belief in God and organized religion.

I was brought up in a strictly religious home. My dad's father was a minister in an extremely conservative church, and my parents were both Christian and insisted we attend church from the time we were born. We attended services

Part Two: The Mama and Papa Wolves

three times a week without fail, twice on Sunday and once on Wednesdays for Bible study.

Even though I was forced to attend church from the time I could walk, I had always felt like I was just going through the motions. I did love the music, especially when my dad sang. He had an angelic bass voice that brought the congregation to tears every time he sang. My mom, sister, and I all sang in the choir regularly, as well.

Aside from the music, though, it never felt right to me. The people seemed insincere. I knew many of them well enough to know the way they behaved on Sunday was nothing like who they were during the week. Some of them didn't behave that well on Sundays, either! It seemed like a house full of hypocrites to me. But my disillusionment with the superficial, hypocritical behavior of churchgoers was just the tip of the iceberg.

The bigger issue was I never believed in God. Religion had always been forced on me. I didn't feel what they all said I was supposed to feel. I didn't find comfort in the lessons offered up in the Bible passages. Even prayers felt forced and contrived. Surely there must be something more, I thought. Something that would resonate with me and make more sense. When I learned about the science of evolution in school, that clicked for me. I was so curious to know more, I checked out some books from the local library about Darwin's theories, which led me to more books about atheism and other beliefs that fell well outside the narrow view of the world and religion that I had known all my life. I realized there must be more answers in the world around me.

I often went with my friend, Gina, to her friend, Sandy's house, which is where I met her hippie parents. They didn't just look and dress differently, they were wild and free-spirited. You could hear it in the way they spoke to their kids and see it in their actions. It was definitely evident any time the subject of church came up.

Sometimes, they'd invite us to stay for dinner, and it was there that I was introduced to the concept of freedom of speech within a family. They not only allowed discussions about controversial topics, they also instigated and encouraged them. I was in awe. They described how you could be a spiritual, moral person without believing in God or subscribing to formal religion. They called it the "church of life." This was the ideal I was searching for. *This made sense to me.*

Besides the eye-opening, world-expanding ideas they shared and the great example of a more open family culture than I'd ever known, Sandy's mom also had long, wavy, wild hair that she had dyed reddish-brown. She was the first woman I'd ever met with red hair, besides my grandmother, and it was the first time I started to think that maybe having curly, red hair might actually be kind of cool. It was liberating.

Unfortunately, when I tried to talk about my doubts with my parents, I was immediately shut down. I tried to explain my thoughts and feelings about religion but was met with dismissive rejection. I was looking for guidance and encouragement, instead all I got was criticism and accusations. I thought, *Isn't this what teenagers were supposed to do? Isn't it just part of evolving and discovering who you want to be?* Not in our house. We just did *not* talk about things, anything. We didn't talk about our feelings. We weren't encouraged to be curious, form our own opinions, or make decisions for ourselves. We were taught to follow orders and do as we were told. We were subject to their control, their rules. We were told what to believe, think, say and do. How to dress, talk, and act. So, my expressions of doubt and wondering were received as an absolute assault on my parents' authority. I was deemed disrespectful, disobedient, and rebellious, which truthfully was nothing new for me. I was reminded again that I *was* the black sheep of the family, after all.

In addition to the long list of grievances my parents already had with me, this latest "affront" pushed them to take action. I was given a choice: I could go live with my grandmother in Idaho or stay with my parents with the agreement that I would enroll in the Christian school that had just opened at the church we attended, for fall. The idea of a small, Christian based school didn't excite me. I knew it was their way of trying to exert further control, to force their religious ideals on me and "fix" me.

I figured life with my grandmother would be more of an oppressive nightmare than I already had with my parents, and I thought that with the school being so close to home, about a mile, and a few of my friends were also going to attend, it might not be so bad. So I opted to stay. If they'd offered to send me to my great-grandparents, however, I would have jumped at the chance. That would have been some serious history repeating itself, since my mother had gone to live with them as teenager, as well. But unfortunately, they were too old by now, both experiencing declining health.

The next fall, I started at the Christian school as agreed. It was a very small school, only about thirty students between middle and high school. The second year, they added another fifteen students in a separate elementary class, where I got the chance to do some student teaching for class credit, an opportunity I likely would not have had at the public high school.

My best friends, Kelly and Gina, attended as well, which made it more bearable. It was structured as a kind of one-room schoolhouse. If we needed to study more challenging subjects, we had to go take them over at the public high school nearby which I did for advanced math and science.

It was kind of boring, but honestly, I didn't mind. I didn't care that much about school anymore and had really lost interest at that point. The high standards set by my teachers in Munich had changed my expectations completely. I gave up on the hope of having engaging, inspiring teachers now that we were back in Washington, and was happy just to kill time and push through it until graduation. During my sophomore year, I got into a serious relationship, which became more of my focus for the last couple of years of school. That and figuring out how to live alone.

Just before the fall of my sophomore year, when I was due to begin at the new school, my parents moved to an apartment about an hour away from my neighborhood in Washington, without warning or explanation. This made getting to and from school difficult because I had to take three different buses each way, which took me over an hour. That meant I had to leave the house at 6 a.m., just to get to school on time. Even though the situation was dramatically different than what I had agreed to, I still felt that it wasn't worse than the alternative. At least I wasn't living in a small town in Idaho with my grandmother!

What *was* worse than changing schools, however, was living in a camper by myself, parked outside their new two-

Part Two: The Mama and Papa Wolves

bedroom apartment because there wasn't room for me. I wish I had asked my dad before he died why they had moved to that apartment. I'll never know why they chose an apartment with no room for me. Had they really expected me, as a sixteen-year-old young woman, to share a room with my fifteen-year-old brother?

I have a feeling, even if I could have gotten an answer, there just wouldn't be any explanation that would undo the pain this experience caused me. I knew they were unhappy with me, I knew they had wanted to send me away. I knew they blamed me for all their problems, all our family's problems. But there's just no other way to say it other than this—it was just plain cruel.

Any anger that had been building in me, along with any frustrations, or disappointments were reinforced and this had confirmed what I'd already felt was true for so long—that I had been abandoned by them emotionally. I was on my own. I would somehow have to find a way to fulfill my own basic needs, both physical and emotional.

At that time, my sister had left home to attend college, and my brother was living in his own world, oblivious to what was going on in mine. He was having some trouble at school and dabbling in illegal activities (which I didn't know about until years later), and there was no one else to help me. It was up to me. Everything I had learned about the world while living in Munich, all the independence and self-sufficiency I'd realized I had within me, became my essential resource for pulling myself up.

This experience taught me the valuable life lesson that it doesn't matter how far you fall, it's how you pull yourself back up that matters. No one is going to do it for you. You've got to dig deep and make it happen for yourself.

Lil' Red

This became a lesson I would be reminded of and draw upon many more times in my life.

I had already seen that lesson in action, or rather the evidence of the opposite: what happens when someone is not capable of pulling themselves up. In the year before we moved to the new apartment, my mom's youngest sister moved into a house nearby us, presumably so she could be closer to my mom for support. There were discussions about her and her two young kids possibly living with us, but it was ultimately decided it was better for her to have her own place.

She lived a few blocks away from us, in a rundown, neglected old bungalow that outwardly resembled my aunt's life—dirty and messy, with a neglected, overgrown yard, distressed paint, and broken windows. She had been married to an abusive alcoholic, on welfare and disability income for her mental illness for years.

At one point, she had her children taken away from her by protective services, since she'd neglected them so severely endangering their health. The neglect was obvious from the first time I met her kids, when they were three and one years old. I was just twelve at the time. The one-year-old was stiff as a board and just lay motionless in her crib. Even at twelve years old, I knew enough to know there was something seriously wrong with the little girl, that this wasn't normal.

By the time she'd moved near us, my aunt had recently regained custody of her children. She was separated from their abusive, alcoholic father and was trying to start a new life on her own.

I volunteered to stop by her house most days after school, wanting to help her with the kids and doing whatever I could around the house. Usually, when I arrived, the kids were running around in dirty diapers that had clearly not been changed for hours. They hadn't been fed and were in desperate need of attention.

I did everything I could to help those poor, innocent kids, my cousins. I bathed them, fed them, and loved on them as much as I could. I would often find furniture or toys out at the curb and clean them up to give them. I even made some simple clothes for them on my sewing machine since she didn't have money to buy them.

Despite her intentions, my aunt continued to neglect her children. Whether she didn't really want to change or ultimately just wasn't capable, I don't know. It was heartbreaking. When my parents moved away to the new apartment, I wasn't able to visit anymore.

She ended up marrying a man from our church, from one of the "good" families, whose dad was one of the church leaders. That "good church-going guy" turned out, sadly, to also be abusive.

Witnessing her struggle firsthand had a profound effect on me as a young teenager. I could see how when someone either refused to change their behavior and circumstances, or just wasn't able to, that it had repercussions not just to their life but also to those around them.

No amount of help from me or anyone else made a difference because the desire to change didn't come from within her. She wouldn't or couldn't pull herself back up.

That experience made me determined that I would not end up the same way.

Although I now faced the biggest challenge of my life so far, having to figure out how to live independently from my parents, I felt confident that my resilience, my grit and

Lil' Red

determination, coupled with my fuck-you gene, would ensure my survival.

Part Two: The Mama and Papa Wolves

Chapter 12

Looking Back

I BELIEVE THAT LOOKING at our past and digging up pain and trauma absolutely has value. Our family history is relevant in that it provides information about the unresolved trauma and stress that is passed on through our genes from one generation to the next. We can't just put all our pain and trauma in little boxes and set them aside. We can pretend all we want, ignore them and "tuck" them away. But the reality is they're all still there, affecting us on a very deep level.

When I was in my early forties, after my divorce from my second husband of twenty years, I had the great privilege of being counseled by a wonderful therapist in Boulder. That counselor taught me about going all the way through painful moments, rather than setting them aside or trying to cover over them. He taught me that, when we have painful experiences, if we step away from the moment rather than working through it, we're left with that exact pain we're experiencing in that moment. That's what sticks with us. We hold *that* pain, *that* trauma, and we carry that around. And although we think we've cleverly pushed it to our subconscious and believe it is not something we feel every day, it actually sits there and festers like rotten fruit, ready to burst back into the present whenever there's any kind of trigger or perceived threat.

The alternative action is to stop and face the moment, to work your way *through* it and come out the other side. By doing that, even if it means temporarily experiencing more emotion, more pain, it leaves you on the other side of it. Then that other feeling is what you're left with. If you've done it right, it is a feeling of resolution, peace, comfort, and understanding, maybe even forgiveness. It is much healthier to be stacking up *those* feelings than the festering, rotting ones.

A great example of this happened to me when I was filing for that same divorce. It was a beautiful, sunny summer day in Colorado and I'd just come out of the courthouse in Boulder after filing the papers to initiate the divorce. I sat down in my car and was crying. Without thinking, I reached over to grab my phone and look for missed messages.

I caught myself in that moment, stepping away from the pain. Instead, I set my phone down and drove up into the foothills, where I sat by the side of a lake and reflected on the moment. I realized I wasn't sad because I was getting a divorce which was my first thought. I knew I didn't regret that decision. I figured out that I was sad because I had to let go of my idea of what I thought my future would hold and accept the reality of what it was going to be. I also felt sad that our separation had hurt our children. I acknowledged for myself that the task that lay ahead of me, of reinventing my life, rebuilding a new definition of our family, and redefining myself, was why I felt sad and overwhelmed. Those realizations meant that I came out the other side of the pain and sadness. If I hadn't taken the time to process it, I would have forever associated sadness with the moment of filing for divorce. Instead, I found peace, even though I knew what lay ahead was a difficult road.

Going back to when I was in my early thirties, I was catapulted into a deep dive of my family history after my father's death. After finding resolution, peace, and forgiveness with him before he died, which I've already shared about, I decided it was worth the effort to try to do the same with my mother. While there were similar issues of abandonment, there was also fear, anger, and the years of physical and emotional abuse to address. Looking at it through the new lens of adulthood and motherhood, with three young children of my own, I could see her life, her family history, and other factors that had contributed to my abuse with a more sympathetic and understanding heart.

When I looked back at her troubled childhood, the abuse *she* had suffered, her family history, and what she went through being such a young mother with so many demands and pressures, and added in the continual absences of my father, it made me feel like I wished I could go back to that time and just hug her. I told her how I could see she was trying to make a better life for herself and for us than what she had had growing up. I told her I could see that she had done the best she could and how she had done so many things right. I also told her that ultimately I didn't condone the abuse, but I *could* understand where it came from.

She responded by opening up to me about how hard those times were for her, especially when we were younger. She admitted that even she didn't understand why she took her anger out on me the way she did. And she *apologized*. It was one of the most powerful moments of my life. As was the moment of forgiveness that followed. I hadn't asked for it, hadn't expected it and hadn't even realized how much I needed it until it happened, both her apology and my forgiveness.

After her husband's tragic death, when all her mental health disorders surfaced, I tried desperately to be part of my mother's life and include her in mine. Sadly, when I was in my mid-thirties, after years of suffering emotional abuse from her to the point of it being detrimental to my own mental and physical health, I was forced to make one of the most difficult decisions of my life: the decision to sever all ties with my mother completely and permanently, in order to save myself. I could no longer allow the abuse in my life, and this was my only way out. This time, though, *I chose* to break free of her. I was especially grateful I made this effort when I did, to resolve my feelings and address the pain she'd caused me in childhood.

I've only spoken to her twice in the twenty-five years since then. Once was after my brother died, I reached out to her with a handwritten letter to share my sympathy, compassion, and condolences for her deep sorrow from that loss. The other was when I was visiting friends near Bellingham where she was living at the time, and my sister happened to be visiting my mom at the same time.

Although I hadn't spoken to my mom for nearly fifteen years at that point, she encouraged me to join her at my mother's house for dinner. Let's just say, it didn't go well. She hardly recognized me and barely said a word to me. So, I decided to leave that door closed. I have no regret, only a wistful sadness and wish that it could have ended differently. But having had our moment of resolution that

Part Two: The Mama and Papa Wolves

resulted in forgiveness, I had let go of the hope of a different past and accepted my fate of living out the rest of my life without a mother.

Looking back to my family history, I can see the influences over generations that came together to make me who I am. Not just the pain and trauma, the struggles, trials, and tribulations, but also the fortitude, grit, resilience, and determination to seek a better life, as well. Gammy who survived the journey west in a covered wagon when so many did not. My mother, Darlene, who survived a dysfunctional and troubled family, and her own abuse, who went on to make a better life for herself. My father, Roger, who survived the hardships of war and years of service in the military. These powerful genetics, both good and bad, came together to forge the feisty, rambunctious, fearless, adventurous, red-headed unicorn that I am, armed with determination, resilience, persistence, tenacity, grit, and a truckload of fuck-you gene.

I needed every bit of those reserves and ammunition for my biggest battle in life, the one that tested me more than any other, that took me to the brink of death—the battle of Lil' Red vs. the Big, Bad Wolf.

Lil' Red

PART THREE
The Big, Bad Wolf

*When you find your most broken self,
that's when you find your strongest self, too.*

Lil' Red

Part Three: The Big, Bad Wolf

Chapter 13

Teasing the Wolf

AS I GOT OUT OF HIS baby-blue '79 Monte Carlo, I coyly left one of my shoes down on the floor, where he couldn't see it, then slammed the heavy car door and shouted "Bye! Thanks for the lift!" over my shoulder, as I ran into the house without looking back.

It was a warm summer Wednesday night, which at our house, meant we were at church. This particular night, I had gone with my friend, Kelly, to her church instead of ours, over in Puyallup which was about thirty minutes away. She and I were part of a singing group that performed at different churches and events and our ensemble sang at her church that night.

After our performance, we were all hanging around in the teen "lounge," which was really just an open area where they'd put some old couches and bean bags to encourage teens to hang out there (supervised, of course), rather than in other places where they might get into trouble.

The tall, handsome youth pastor came over to talk to us and immediately caught my attention. He was much younger than most of the other church leaders. And he was *cute*. So tall, maybe 6'5"? I wasn't sure. He was obviously very fit, had a great smile, brown, wavy hair, and brown eyes. Not my usual type, I usually liked blond, blue-eyed boys, but he was handsome. And so not a boy. This guy had swagger.

I decided to flirt with him a little and was surprised when he obviously started flirting back. He left us, going on to talk with some of the other teens who were chatting and laughing with him, but I could feel the heat of his gaze from across the room. I pretended not to notice. But I definitely noticed, and so did my friend, Kelly.

She sidled up to me and whispered in my ear, "He's single."

"Who?" I asked, as I pushed her away dismissively.

"Larry, the youth pastor," she replied, tilting her head towards him.

"Don't be silly! He's probably way too old for me," I quipped back.

It was obvious he was older, although I wasn't exactly sure how much. I thought to myself, *"Why would someone like that ever be interested in me?"*

I was just sixteen, with wild, frizzy red hair that I tried desperately to straighten every day, fighting against my natural curl. I wasn't pretty in the popular-cheerleader kind of way, but in more of a natural way. I certainly didn't have a lot of confidence or self-esteem, and I didn't think I was that attractive even to boys my own age. My parents didn't allow me to date officially, but I secretly had had a boyfriend for several months when I was fourteen and had been with a couple of other boys but hadn't really had much actual dating experience. I was pretty sure this handsome,

Part Three: The Big, Bad Wolf

confident, fully adult, independent, grown *man* would never look twice at me.

But he did. More than twice. He circled back around after a while to talk to me again. I had taken off my shoes, which were heels, something I wasn't used to wearing and were killing me. Still very much the tomboy, I was always more comfortable in tennis shoes or flats. I had just made myself comfortable on one of the couches in the lounge when he came over and asked if he could sit next to me. I nervously agreed.

He quickly put me at ease with his charm and humor. The conversation between us flowed easily about a variety of things—our interests, hobbies, favorite foods, and just general chitchat. He told me that he was in the army but would be getting out in a couple of years, because he planned to go back to college to play basketball, something he was very passionate about.

After a while, the group started to thin and people were going home. I looked around for Kelly since she was my ride but couldn't find her anywhere. Another friend told me she'd left, which meant I was stuck and would have to call my parents to come get me.

Larry overheard the whole conversation and offered me a ride home, saying he was going that way anyway. I found out later that this was absolutely not true, that the base housing where he lived was in the completely opposite direction. I readily accepted and slid into his baby-blue muscle car, bare feet and all. I was kind of into cars, as I've mentioned, through my dad's passion for old cars, so I was definitely impressed by his car, especially since most of the guys I knew drove their parents' cars or old beaters. I could see that Larry took pride in his car, and he told me all about

Lil' Red

it and how he was into muscle cars, something else we had in common.

On the way home, we had the windows down and listened to his favorite music, Creedence Clearwater Revival, on a cassette tape. Our conversation continued to flow easily during the thirty-minute ride home, and by the time we reached my house, I had already decided I wanted to see him again. That was when I devised the plan to "accidentally" leave one of my shoes in his car Cinderella style. I had them in my hand, so it was easy to just slide one down under the edge of the seat and leave it there as I got out.

It worked. The next day, he got my number from Kelly and called to ask if he could bring my shoe back to me the next week at church. It wasn't my regular church, but I eagerly agreed to be back there the next Wednesday. We spent a couple more hours talking on the phone that night. I stretched the long phone cord as far as it would go, so I could sit in privacy in my favorite hiding place, my dad's music closet. From then on, our relationship was a bit of a whirlwind.

After I got my Cinderella shoe back, we started to secretly see each other a couple of times a week and talked on the phone just about every day. We both agreed that since we were sure my parents and his church wouldn't approve of us dating, mostly because he was the youth pastor, but also because of the age difference, we should keep it under wraps for a while. He often came to pick me up after school when my parents thought I was hanging out with friends, and we'd go off somewhere and grab a bite to eat or just sit in his car or at a park and talk.

Part Three: The Big, Bad Wolf

The strong physical gravitational pull between us was hard to ignore, and we didn't waste much time getting around to having sex. I'd already had sex many times with other boys and I was actually the one who initiated it, which surprised (and delighted) him. I think a big part of the excitement was that it was forbidden. In our church, sex was considered sinful outside of marriage. There was also the issue of me being under eighteen, so definitely not legal. But we didn't care about any of that—we did it anyway. A lot. I didn't know anything about birth control or protection, but I deferred to him since he was the older, more experienced of us. He assured me that pulling out, even though not as satisfying for him, was effective. I realized later that I was just plain lucky that it worked.

Over the six months or so that we were secretly dating, he called me about once a week on our home phone. Each time, I stretched the cord to the closet again and sat there talking with him until one of my parents kicked me off for tying up the house phone for too long. It became obvious to them that I was seeing someone. They finally insisted on meeting him.

That's when the shit hit the fan.

Chapter 14

Life Shifts

SHOCKED TO SEE A grown man of almost thirty rather than a teenager, my parents were concerned and displeased, to say the least, when Larry rolled up and stepped out of his car.

I'd invited him for dinner, but we never made it to the dinner table. My dad stepped outside to greet him, had a few stern words with him, then he came back inside and said, "He needs to leave. He's not welcome in this house."

Larry got back in his car but hadn't left yet. My dad said he felt it was inappropriate for us to be dating. He proclaimed, "It's my house, my rules," and "As long as you're under my roof, you will abide by them."

It didn't matter to him that Larry was a youth pastor or that he was in the army like my dad, or even that he seemed to be a good guy. All that mattered, all they could see, was that he was twelve years older, which, I admit, was an extreme age difference and highly unusual. But the fact that they wouldn't even listen to my side of it really pissed me off.

Part Three: The Big, Bad Wolf

I strongly declared my feelings, saying, "I'm in love with him, and if you don't like it, then I'll just leave. You can keep your damn roof and shove it up your ass!" I dramatically marched right out the front door with nothing but the clothes on my back and my purse in hand. Maybe not the smartest move, but the sixteen-year-old me thought so at the time.

Looking back, I wish my dad had gone back inside and gotten one of his many guns. I wish he'd threatened Larry and told him he would have him arrested if he ever came near me again. I wish he'd pulled rank and used his position as an officer in the army to somehow force Larry to leave me alone. I wish he'd have done *something* more. Both of my parents—wasn't it their job to protect me? Why didn't they try harder? I'll never know. Instead, they did nothing. They just let me go.

I'm not saying I blame them for the misery that would come later as a result of my choices, but I do wish they'd tried harder to intervene then. I honestly think they were so mired down in their own "relationshit," they couldn't muster the energy to do anything more. For whatever reason, on that day, they let me walk out the door.

A few months later, when my sister left home to go to college, my parents moved from our house in Spanaway, Washington to an apartment about forty-five minutes away. My guess is they did this for financial reasons, but at the time no explanation was offered to me. There were a couple of major problems with this for me.

The first was that the private Christian school they had forced me to attend was now forty-five minutes away, or more than an hour by bus. Sending me there had been their way of getting me "under control," to fix me, but, at the time

I agreed to go, we lived five minutes from it. While I had my driver's license by that time, I didn't have my own car, so I was expected to make this trek by bus to and from school each day.

The second problem with their move was that the small apartment they chose only had two bedrooms, one for my parents and one very small room presumably for me and my fifteen-year-old brother to share. I hadn't wanted to share a room with him in the last house, and now that we were a couple of years older, I certainly didn't want to share with him then. This was the second time they'd chosen a living situation that made me feel unwanted, like there wasn't a place for me and I hadn't been considered at all.

As a solution, my dad offered up his camping trailer for me which he parked in the parking lot just outside our apartment. I had been sleeping out there for a couple of months, essentially living on my own, when the Larry situation exploded. So, when I marched out of the house that day, it wasn't much of a stretch in my mind to think I just wouldn't be living at home at all anymore.

The problem now was where *would* I live? I reached out to my close friend back in Spanaway. She was an only child, and her family lived in a bigger house than ours, one with a couple of spare bedrooms. I asked if it would be okay for me to live with them for a few months, until school was out for the summer, to buy myself time to form another, more permanent plan. Her mother agreed. Unfortunately, after only two months with them, I realized how incredibly controlling and mean her mother actually was. She tried to force me to do everything her way, from organizing my clothes and room to how I dressed and talked, even what I ate. It was so extreme. When I pushed back about it, she

Part Three: The Big, Bad Wolf

became verbally abusive, yelling at me and threatening to kick me out. I told her I already had that kind of relationship with my own parents and if I was going to be treated that way, I'd just move back home. She helped me pack.

Since Larry lived in the barracks on base, I couldn't live with him. Otherwise, I would have. Next, I went and stayed with my friend, Gina, and her family for a month, but her parents belonged to the same church we did and sided with my parents on the issue of me dating Larry, which created a great deal of tension. They also knew him personally from a couple of years before, when they had attended the same church as him in Puyallup. I was back to square one. With no other real options, I decided to move back into my dad's camper.

On the one hand, I liked the privacy it afforded me. It was my very own space, which I'd fixed up just the way I liked it, with lots of soft, cozy blankets and pillows (including my favorite quilt from my grandmother), some of my favorite cow things, and even a small, lime-green rug on the floor to brighten it up. My dad even hooked up the propane tank so I could cook for myself. I only went inside their apartment to use the bathroom and shower. Otherwise, I was on my own.

I was gone most of the time, spending time with Larry after school when I wasn't at my job at Burger King. Since I had my own income, I bought all my own clothes, food, and other necessities. I even bought myself a little thirteen-inch black-and-white TV. I was saving money for my own car, but my dad let me use his little Datsun about once a week to go back and forth to work, if I paid for the gas. He knew how much I liked driving it even though it was kind of an old beater. Still, it *was* a manual transmission, and I loved it.

As lonely as it was, living out in that camper on my own, I relished the break from fighting with my parents over Larry. I didn't fully realize it at the time, but they were having very serious marital problems, had been for years, and were headed for divorce, which finally came just after I graduated.

I was so sick and tired of them blaming all our family's problems on me. They told me repeatedly how I was the black sheep of our family and how what they called my rebellious behavior was causing all the discord in our family. Their list of my offenses was long, including swearing, missing curfew, lying about wrecking the family car, wearing inappropriate clothing, rejecting our religion, and now dating someone they didn't approve of. I'm not denying that I was guilty on all charges, I definitely was. I just don't think I deserved the blame for *ALL* our family's problems.

And those offenses were just the things they knew about. There was more. *Much* more.

If they had known all of what I'd actually been up to since about the age of fourteen, I think they'd have sent me away or maybe tried to have me arrested. My friend, Gina, my main partner in crime, was a wonderfully devious soul with whom I connected on a deep level. We just *got* each other, we were two peas in a pod. Same sense of humor, same sense of adventure, same irreverent attitude toward church and God, same distrust of authority.

We got up to some serious mischief together. We used to do sleepovers at her house and would wait until around 10 p.m., when her parents were sound asleep, then quietly switch the garage door to manual mode, lift it open, and roll their car out of the garage and down the driveway. Once we

Part Three: The Big, Bad Wolf

were far enough away, she'd kick on the ignition, and away we went! We usually went to visit friends from other schools, mostly cute guys, or to a school football game and then to a party at someone's house. Then, around 1:00 or 2:00 a.m., after cleverly remembering to fill the car with gas and cleaning it up, we'd roll it back into the garage, close the door, and crash in her bed until morning. We were only fourteen, and neither of us even had a permit—but that didn't stop us!

I didn't do drugs. I didn't commit any criminal offenses (okay, with the exception of driving without a license), and I did nothing more than a lot of other teenagers do—partying, a bit of drinking, and sneaking out. Outside the confines of our religion, my swearing, way of dressing, breaking curfew, and even the occasional lying all fell within normal teenage behavior. I was really just a very troubled soul in search of my place in the world, seeking meaning to my life, acceptance, security, and love.

That's where Larry came in.

For nearly two years since we'd been together, he had been supportive, encouraging, loving, and attentive. He listened. He validated my feelings. He understood me. I felt good, alive, energized, and positive around him. He was my escape from all my problems. So, on my eighteenth birthday, a rare sunny day in the soggy Northwest, when he took me out for a nice dinner, got down on one knee, and proposed—I immediately accepted!

I graduated high school on June 5 that year with high marks but little pomp or circumstance. Then, I quietly left town for Kansas with Larry. We were married six days later, in a small, simple ceremony on a sticky-hot day, me in an inexpensive, long, lacy, Gunne Sax dress and him in a rented baby-blue tuxedo.

We'd been together nearly two years, during which time he had seemed to be my knight in shining armor, the one who would save me from the misery of life that I had known for the last few years. But that shine wore off almost immediately after the wedding, and what was underneath was a Big Bad Wolf whom I would have to face alone.

Part Three: The Big, Bad Wolf

Chapter 15

The Tables Are Turned

JUNE 11, 1983, OUR WEDDING day, marked the beginning of the loss of my feelings of confidence and self-worth, of feeling loved, safe, and secure. To be honest, I don't think I ever really had all of those, but Larry had made me *think* I did. I just didn't know that yet.

Although this false sense of security had provided a cushion for me and given me a sense of security for years, I could no longer live in denial about how the world wasn't a horrible place with horrible people in it. I still held the belief that people were essentially good. Was that actually denial? I don't think so. That's something we choose, even if just subconsciously. No, it was more naïveté. Either way, this was the day when I suddenly shifted into a new reality.

Through the hardships of the last few years, and even back to the time when I was being bullied at school and abused by my mother, my fuck-you gene had kept me going. I honestly don't think I would have survived to see my eighteenth birthday without it. However, its light was to be extinguished over the next year, drowned in misery, only to be re-lit in my darkest moment.

Lil' Red

I think I should stop here to explain something: the thing I refer to as my "fuck-you gene," which is a phrase coined years ago by a close friend of mine to explain our ability to get ourselves out of bad situations. Some people call it resilience or fortitude, determination, gumption, or tenacity. It's actually all of those things. Whether it's genetic, something you're born with, or something you learn, I don't know. I think mine mostly came with my red hair, maybe some genetics, but I think I also learned how to harness it over the years. Whatever it is, it's the thing that saved my ass — many times.

Shortly after the wedding, within two weeks to be exact, Larry had shifted from a loving, supportive, encouraging partner to a moody, distant, and angry one. The charming, attentive, funny, engaging Larry I had known was gone, *except* when we were out in public.

We'd moved to Olathe, Kansas, so he could go back to college after several years in the Army to play basketball for the college there. Although I didn't know anyone in Kansas, Larry had a few friends who had also recently moved to Olathe. The change in climate was the biggest adjustment for me, honestly, even more than moving away from family and friends. I wasn't close to my family at the time, and since I had grown up moving every couple of years and having to leave friends behind, that was nothing new for me. The heat, though — *ugh*. I'd take a shower, and by the time I dried off, I'd be dripping with sweat again. And the bugs! *So many bugs!* We had roaches in our apartment as big as my thumb!

At first, he just seemed to make a big thing out of small things. One night I overcooked the hamburgers I had made for dinner. It made him angry and as he pushed one of the dining chairs over, he yelled at me, "How could you be so stupid? What is the matter with you?" He later apologized for yelling at me saying that he was just stressed and overly hungry.

Another afternoon when I was making lemonade, he commented that I was "*Doing it all wrong,*" and again stated how stupid I must be. As I reached into the freezer for ice, he slammed the door on my arm and hand. I yanked my bruised arm back in shock, retreated to the bedroom, and cried. That time he didn't try to console me or offer any apology.

Another time, I had come home late from work and rushed to make dinner for him, because he was already mad that I was late. We had nothing else in the fridge, so I could only manage a casserole of potatoes and hot dogs with cheese on it. I was proud of myself that I had thrown it together so quickly and with what little we had.

He tasted it, called it slop he wouldn't feed a dog, and threw the entire dish against the wall. Then he stormed out of the house to go meet a friend for a beer, while I spent an hour cleaning up the broken glass and casserole off the floor and wall.

With each passing week, Larry's anger and yelling became more intense and more frequent. The physical abuse escalated, as well, from pushing things, banging his fist on the wall, or shaking it at me to *actually* pushing me and hitting me. I never knew what would set him off, so I couldn't even adjust my behavior in order to avoid it. Nothing I did was right. This was an all-too-familiar feeling for me.

He also began telling me regularly how I was worthless and good for nothing, how lucky I was to have him because no one else would want me. I thought this was interesting because I was obviously good enough to provide income for both of us from my meager salary at McDonald's, although I wouldn't dare say that to his face. He even complained about that, saying it was a pathetic, disgusting job for losers and that I stunk from it every day when I came home. (That part was true and, sadly, unavoidable.) I was too afraid to stand up for myself, to point out that if I weren't working at my loser job, we wouldn't have any income at all. Where had my fuck-you gene gone? What had happened to my spunk, my fighting spirit? It seemed to be drowning in fear.

None of it felt right. On some level, I knew it wasn't. I felt like I had a dark cloud of sadness, despair, and fear over me all the time. I didn't sleep well, so I was tired all the time. I had gone from being a feisty, energetic, athletic, outgoing person to someone who barely acknowledged those around me. And I was afraid to defend myself against him. I do think the fact that I already had low self-esteem after all of those years of childhood bullying and the abuse from my mother played a role. It felt kind of like being behind the eight ball, like somehow, he honed in on my weaknesses and insecurities and was destroying me from the inside out.

In general, I felt like I'd had a lot more life experience than most girls my age, but I was still naïve in so many ways. Even though I'd experienced abuse from my Mama Wolf, that was under the guise of discipline. I honestly had no idea there were people in the world who had these kinds of relationships, especially as newlyweds. I had seen my parents have countless arguments over the years, but it was never like this. My father never raised a hand or even gestured toward my mother in anger. I had no idea that the

Part Three: The Big, Bad Wolf

things I was experiencing were all red flags of an abusive partner or even that such a thing existed.

I thought of it as a "Jekyll and Hyde" persona. Larry was so charming and gregarious, often the center of attention and life of the party, out in public. But he turned into a vicious, angry, Big Bad Wolf behind closed doors. He created a world where he was the sole provider of my emotional needs. He isolated me from friends and family and then systematically destroyed my self-esteem with negative comments and constant criticism. The use of force to exert dominance and control was something I should have recognized from the abuse by my mother, but I didn't put two and two together. Maybe because he was my husband and had been so loving and attentive the first couple of years we were together, I didn't realize he was doing the same thing my Mama Wolf had done to me for most of my childhood. And more.

As time passed, Larry also became increasingly jealous and possessive. Any time I was late coming home from work or took longer than he thought I should at the grocery store or running errands, he would accuse me of being unfaithful and scream at me, "Who were you with? Tell me, you slut!" The more I tried to explain or defend myself, the angrier he became.

I soon figured out it was better just to let him rant, to deal with the lashing that came with it, and to retreat afterward, knowing he would come to me a couple of hours later and offer up what seemed to be a sincere apology. Those apologies also came with blame—it was *my* fault he was angry, *my* fault he had to hit me. And I started to believe it all. I know it must seem impossible for someone looking at it objectively from the outside. The only thing I can equate it to is that it's a kind of brainwashing that happens, so slowly you don't even realize it.

One night, Larry was furious about the fact that I'd left a couple of dirty dishes in the sink. As he started to yell at me about it, he picked them up, saying, "Apparently you don't give a shit about the dishes, so fuck it," and he threw them against the wall. I felt my heart breaking just like each fractured dish as it hit the floor.

My pulse was racing, and I could see this was escalating quickly. I tried to apologize and get away from him, quickly heading toward the stairs to our room. He blocked me from going up, and before I knew what was happening, his fist was coming straight for my face.

I managed to dodge the blow, but his fist went right into the wall next to my head. He was even more mad now.

"You fucking bitch! I need that hand for basketball!" he screamed, as if his hitting the wall instead of my face was *my* fault. When he grabbed his hand, bent over in pain, I made a run for the front door.

I ran across the street to the neighbors' house and used their phone to call the police. The police arrived several minutes later to find me on the front doorstep still scared and crying, and a much calmer Larry inside, icing his hand. I explained what had happened and even showed them the hole in the wall and his bloodied fist. He denied any wrong doing, of course.

They told me there was nothing they could do, because they hadn't actually *seen* it happen. I was astounded. I had finally tried to get real help, but it had failed.

Since I was isolated from any friends or family and got no help from the police, the only people I had left to turn to were the elders in our church. I met with the pastor, and he

Part Three: The Big, Bad Wolf

assured me that all newlywed couples have problems, it was all very normal and it would work itself out. I just had to be patient and "be a better wife," he said. He quoted some Bible verses to make his point, which was that I needed to try harder.

Larry was also very apologetic and remorseful each time, saying "I just don't know what gets into me. I'll do better, I promise."

So, I stayed. I tried. I waited and hoped for better. I shifted into a life of walking on eggshells, trying desperately to do everything just right but never knowing when or why the next incident would come, when he would explode in anger.

One night, Larry pushed me so hard, I fell back over the arm of the couch and crashed down onto the glass coffee table, shattering it into pieces. This scared both of us, and he was immediately backpedaling, apologizing and again promising it would never happen again.

This time, I tried to leave. This was the most violent he had been so far, and I was really scared. I went and stayed for a few nights with a friend from church, to give him time to cool down and me time to figure out what to do.

He talked to the pastor at church and said he had "renewed his commitment to God." He swore this would finally help him get his anger under control. Between his convincing argument and the encouragement of the friend I was staying with, as well as others in the church, I agreed to return home and give him yet another chance.

Then, the unexpected happened.

Chapter 16

Joy Unravels

WE HAD BEEN MARRIED for just over six months when I found out I was pregnant. It turned out my unicorn powers applied to birth control, too. I was apparently part of the two percent who could still get pregnant while on birth control pills. The news came as a great surprise. I was immediately filled with joy and excitement and the anticipation that maybe this would be the thing to turn my life and marriage around. I had *hope*. Surely no one would beat a pregnant woman or cause harm to an unborn child, right?

I had wanted to be a mother since I was six years old, so for me, this was a dream come true. Now I would have my very own little person to love, someone who would love me back unconditionally. I was beyond excited!

Larry was happy about it, too, at first. My joy was clouded by constant morning sickness, but I found ways to work around it and pushed through. At work, I was ravenously hungry and nauseous all at the same time, with the smells of hot fat, burgers, and chemically-infused foods filling my nose. If I had to throw up at work, I'd either

Part Three: The Big, Bad Wolf

excuse myself to the bathroom or, more often than not, just quietly throw up in my mouth, swallow it and keep going, smiling as if nothing had happened. I carried mints around in my pocket to cover up the constant smell of vomit on my breath.

My McDonald's uniform was already super-ugly — brown polyester with orange-and-red trim, and to accommodate my rapidly swelling belly, I had to switch to a maternity version, which was just as ugly, but there was more of it! I didn't care, though. The fact that I had to switch to maternity clothes so early in the pregnancy should have been my first clue, but I had no idea about these things.

I had also just started working at Pizza Hut in the evenings, because we needed the money. Larry claimed he couldn't work because he was too busy with school and basketball. So, I pushed through all the nausea, vomiting, exhaustion, and sore, swollen breasts to work both jobs – McDonalds for a few hours in the morning, and Pizza Hut in the evening. I was just happy to be pregnant. And honestly, more time away from home, away from the abuse, wasn't necessarily a bad thing for me.

I lay in bed at night, dreaming about what my life would be like as a mother. The life I envisioned was filled with love and affection, it would be calm and serene. Bathed in immaturity and naïveté, I didn't stop to consider what would come *after* the birth. In particular, I didn't consider the fact that *I* was the one earning what little income we had. My thoughts were very simply focused on the belief that my life would look different, *feel* different. I was desperate for a change and was pinning all hope on this baby to somehow rescue me from the nightmare I found myself in.

Lil' Red

I did think about how, growing up, I didn't have a mother who'd shown me how to be the kind of mother I wanted to be. I was a little bit worried I would turn out to be like her but felt sure I could do better. I believed my baby would be safe, that things were going to change in our house, that the violence would stop, and this baby would transport us back to the time when we had a fun, loving, supportive relationship. For now, I was standing on the solid ground of hope, right where I needed to be. That ground would soon crumble beneath me, but for the moment, I clung to it for dear life.

As the newness of the pregnancy wore off, Larry became more impatient with me, especially if I had to miss work for being sick, which was often. By the time I was about fourteen weeks along, he was pretty much back to his old angry, abusive self. Everything pissed him off. I was doing everything I could to appease him, working two jobs, making him meals before I left for work, keeping the house clean, and even still giving him sex when he wanted it, although I had no interest at that point, especially with all the nausea, fatigue and abuse. But it wasn't enough, never enough. He always found fault with something and would often be waiting for me when I returned home from work to yell at me about whatever it was that day.

We also never seemed to have enough money for things like groceries or necessities, because he used what little we had to buy things like a motorcycle, tools, clothes, cars, and whatever else I had no idea about. Somehow that was my fault, too. He accused me of keeping aside money from my paychecks for myself or spending more than my allotted $10 per week for groceries or even of lying about being at work, accusing me of being out with friends or other men.

Part Three: The Big, Bad Wolf

He always had a reason to be angry with me, and again, the yelling turned into pushing and hitting.

I was at work one morning just before my nineteenth birthday, at about sixteen weeks along with my swollen belly now in full view, when I started to feel kind of crampy and even noticed a little bit of blood spotting in my underwear. Naturally it worried me, so I left work immediately and drove myself straight to the doctor's office.

They did some tests and an ultrasound and that's when they showed me on the screen—there were actually *two* babies! I was having twins! Double the joy! I couldn't believe my eyes. I knew there were twins in my family on my dad's side, so it wasn't completely surprising, but it was definitely unexpected. It made more sense now, why my belly had grown so big so quickly. The doctor sent me home, said to take a few days off from both jobs and rest, and assured me it would all be fine.

Instead, it all started to unravel.

When I got home and told Larry that I had to take a little time off from work, he lost his shit. He accused me of creating all of it just to get at him and cause him problems and stress. I told him about the news of the twins, which, to my astonishment, only made him *more* mad.

He said, "We can't even afford *one* kid. Now there's two new mouths to feed? And now you can't work, either? What the fuck are we supposed to do?"

I started to cry, saying the doctor had instructed me to rest because of the bleeding, but he didn't believe me. I was so upset, scared, and angered by his reaction, I actually started yelling back. I knew better, but I didn't care. This was about my babies. It *mattered*.

Lil' Red

It escalated quickly, with him throwing things at me and pushing me around, at which point I ran upstairs to lock myself in our bedroom. But he smashed the door in, pushed me to the floor, and then started kicking me, directing his anger right at my stomach. I tried so desperately to protect my babies, but some of the kicks landed square on.

Whether he realized what he had done or he had simply exhausted his anger I don't know, but he suddenly stopped, went downstairs, and turned on the TV. I lay there, crying and shaking for a bit, then finally pulled myself up onto our bed and fell asleep.

A couple of hours later, I woke up in a pool of blood. And the cramps from earlier were now extremely painful, like nothing I'd ever known. I was in so much pain, I couldn't walk. Hell, I was having a hard time getting in a good breath in between the rapid waves of pain. Larry was downstairs with the TV on so loud, he couldn't hear me screaming for him.

I dragged myself from the bed onto the floor, out the door, and slid down the few stairs to the main level. I screamed again. This time he heard me. He came running and when he saw the trail of blood behind me, he knew it was serious. I said I needed an ambulance, but he said we couldn't afford one, so he called his friend to come drive us to the hospital. He put me in the back seat and climbed in the front with his friend.

All the way there, I just kept thinking, *You did this to me. This is all your fault.*

When we got there, I knew in my heart what was happening but didn't want to accept it. Apparently, when you're this far along and miscarry, it's more like giving birth. Your body is having contractions, but since it's not

Part Three: The Big, Bad Wolf

supposed to be happening, it's also working against itself to stop it. So, twice the pain.

I tried to tell the nurses and doctors around me that it was his fault, that he'd been hitting and kicking me. They didn't seem to hear me. They just kept patting my back, saying it was nature's way and sometimes these things happen, it would all be okay. But I knew it wouldn't. Their words went in and left my mind just as quickly as they'd entered. They had no meaning to me, gave me no comfort.

My babies died that night.

They didn't have to tell me. I knew. I had seen them in the bloody mess. I had felt them as they left my body. I just lay there in the hospital bed, crying until I had no more tears. I had never felt so completely alone. There are no words for that depth of pain, sadness, and loss. And he had killed them, but no one cared.

A couple of days later, Larry drove me home from the hospital. He hadn't even had the decency to visit me in the hospital. No one did. When we got home, I walked from the car back into the house with a deep sense of dread and doom, my steps heavy with the loss I had suffered and the physical pain in my body. How could I have felt anything but hopeless?

I didn't know anything about depression. I just knew I couldn't stop crying. I couldn't sleep, even though I was exhausted. I didn't want to eat. I didn't want to do anything. I was also angry—at the world, at my family for abandoning me, at the God I no longer believed in, and especially at Larry. Any hope that had come with being pregnant was destroyed.

Lil' Red

I had tried to get help, to tell the people around me about the abuse—but none came. I had believed that being pregnant would somehow protect me, save me—but it didn't. I lost hope that my life would ever amount to anything more than the misery I was in. All I could see was that I was stuck in this life with no way out. I was tired of trying. There was no sign of my fuck-you gene or of the strength, resilience, and determination that had saved me the last several years. I realized I had been living in the idea of what I hoped life would be, rather than in the reality of what it was. And I knew my babies were truly better off not being born into this life of mine.

That's when I decided to end my misery on my own terms.

I waited until Larry left the house, and I took all the pills I could find. It was a mix of a few tablets of pain meds the hospital had given me and some Tylenol. I didn't write a note, didn't do anything, just lay down on the bed, closed my eyes, and finally felt the pain and misery melt away.

But fate had a different plan. I don't know exactly how long it was, but shortly after I had swallowed the pills, Larry unexpectedly came home to get something he'd forgotten and came into our room. He saw the empty bottles, saw me asleep on the bed, grabbed me by my arms, and shook me awake, screaming, "What the fuck did you do?"

He picked up my already limp body (I was too weak to resist), threw me over his shoulder like a sack of potatoes, and immediately rushed me back to the hospital, where they pumped my stomach. This is not a procedure I would wish on my worst enemy. It is altogether a painful, disgusting, embarrassing experience. You'd think the doctors and nurses would be sympathetic and

Part Three: The Big, Bad Wolf

understanding, but for me, it was just the opposite. They were harsh, judgmental, critical, and dismissive. They had an accusatory tone whenever they addressed me, which made me feel ashamed and worse than I already felt.

Yet another doctor assured me that, "These things happen," and sometimes, after this kind of loss, it's normal for women to feel "despondent." He said I needed to "toughen up" and get over it that I was young and would bounce back quickly. Not exactly the sympathetic, understanding, motivational speech I needed right then.

The pastor of our church came to counsel me at home afterward, and I tried again to tell him why it had happened, about the abuse and Larry hitting and kicking me right in my stomach. This time I was very clear, I didn't hold anything back.

Once more, he assured me that all new couples have problems. "I know Larry is a good man. He's repented for his sins and is working on doing better. You just need some couples counseling," he said.

I was astounded. *Seriously*? He was defending the man who had just killed my babies, playing it down as if we'd just had a little argument over finances or something trivial. This betrayal by the church solidified my belief that there was no God. How could there be? What God would allow such violence? What God would take two innocent lives? What God would abandon someone in their darkest hour? Without family, the church, and now without my babies or anyone by my side, I had the full knowing of being thoroughly and completely *alone*.

What if just one person who heard my story had actually listened? What if one nurse, one doctor, one church elder had taken a minute to talk to me, to try to help me? What if…?

I was fully resigned to the fact that no one gave a shit about me when one of the few friends I'd gotten close with at work heard I was "unwell" (they had no idea what actually happened), and she came to visit me at home. Fortunately, Larry wasn't home at the time, so I decided to finally tell her everything that had been going on, at that point I had nothing more to lose.

She was shocked, speechless, and saddened to the point of tears. When she got her breath back, she said, "I've honestly never known anyone in this kind of situation, but I really think you need to get away from him. I want to help you, if you'll let me."

She was the first person who seemed to have heard me, who stood up for me, and who wasn't completely dismissive about what I was going through. I was so beaten down, so weak, exhausted, and completely hopeless, I felt this was my only option. I decided she was right and reluctantly accepted her help. For the last few years, I really only had myself to rely on, so trusting a friend to help me was new territory for me.

Her plan was that during the next week when I went back to work, I would sneak a few bits of clothing with me. Then, I would just go home with her after work, instead of going home to Larry. We would figure it out from there, she assured me.

The rest of that week passed without any incident. I was growing more anxious, the closer it got to the big day, but also allowed myself to feel a little bit hopeful that our plan might work. When the day finally arrived, I woke up feeling lighthearted and upbeat, allowing myself to think about the possibility of a different life on the other side of fear.

That afternoon, as I began to get ready for work and was putting a few of my things in a small bag, Larry came in and caught me. He grabbed the bag out of my hand and asked, "What the fuck is this?"

I explained that I just needed some clothes to change into after work, but he knew it wasn't true. He started yelling and accusing me of having an affair, saying I was meeting up with someone after work, which was why I needed the change of clothes. I defended myself, saying he was wrong, but he wouldn't stop.

He even pushed me as he yelled, "You're lying!"

In that moment, I decided it was best to just come clean and admit I wasn't planning on coming home that night. I explained how I couldn't take any more of this life since the babies died, and I just needed to get away for a bit.

He looked at me and said, "You want to go away? Fine." Then, he turned around and walked downstairs.

That's odd, I thought. I'd been expecting him to be furious, to threaten me or yell at me, at least. Then I heard crashing noises and ran down to see what he was doing. He was going around the house picking up anything that was mine and smashing it on the floor. He broke my tennis racket over his knee. He ripped up my family photos and smashed the frames. He said, if I was going to leave, I sure as hell wasn't taking anything with me.

I left for work, sobbing and broken just like all my things. I told my friend I couldn't go with her, there was no point. He'd never let me go. I was too afraid of him, too afraid of what else he might do. I didn't want to put her in danger, as well.

Lil' Red

When I got home that night, I passed the reminder of Larry's horrific outburst in the form of a garbage bin out at the curb, full of my broken life on display for everyone to see. Somehow, I was ashamed of this. Ashamed it was happening to me. Ashamed I wasn't strong enough to make it stop. Ashamed my life was so horrible, I didn't want everyone to see it.

The next day, while I was at work, he went and rented a U-Haul trailer and filled it with a few pieces of our furniture, the rest he sold. When I got home, I saw the trailer attached to the crappy old '63 Dodge convertible sedan (the convertible part was permanent since the rooftop was missing).

I went inside to an empty house, and he told me we were moving to Oregon. His plan was for me to drive the Dodge with no roof, towing the trailer behind, and he would follow along on his motorcycle.

He threatened me, saying, if I changed my mind and tried to stay, he would find me and kill me. If he couldn't have me, no one could. He reminded me that no one else would want me anyway.

I believed him on both counts. I was so beaten down, I had no fight left in me. I called to quit both of my jobs, climbed into the Dodge with the stray dog he'd recently adopted on the seat next to me, and cried the entire twenty-seven-hour drive to Portland.

Part Three: The Big, Bad Wolf

Chapter 17

Portland

WE ARRIVED IN PORTLAND on a beautiful, sunny summer day. Our first task was to find a place to live. We had a little money from the stuff Larry had sold before we left Kansas, just enough to secure a small one-bedroom apartment in a little, run-down complex of about fifteen units. Since we'd sold most everything, we just had a mattress on the floor in the living room, which we'd gotten secondhand, and some clothes. We also had one dining chair that we'd found by the curb, but no table.

With my previous work experience, I was able to get a job at the Pizza Hut there almost immediately (although I'd had to lie about why we left Kansas so abruptly). Somehow, I landed a second job teaching aerobics, which was funny because I really had no idea what I was doing or how I even got that job. I'll admit I looked good in the "Jane Fonda" aerobics outfit they provided, complete with a turquoise leotard, a pink belt, and matching leg warmers. Also, I had energy and enthusiasm, apparently that was enough.

I worked teaching in the mornings from 8:00 a.m. until noon, then I went to my job at Pizza Hut from 2:00 p.m. until close. I didn't feel like I had much choice, since Larry claimed, yet again, that he couldn't find work, although it didn't seem to me like he really even tried. Even though I was probably working too much, it was my only escape from a horrible and violent home life.

I quickly settled into a familiar routine of working both jobs and walking on eggshells at home, desperately trying to avoid the minefield of anger and abuse.

My one joy was spending time with the little eight-year-old boy in the apartment at the end of our complex, several doors down from us. I encountered him one day as his mother was taking him out for a walk in his wheelchair. He had cerebral palsy and couldn't walk or talk exactly, but he and I had an instant connection. We communicated just fine.

He would wait at his front door for me to come home from work, and as soon as he saw me getting out of my car, he would start to wail and scream with excitement for me to come visit him, which I did daily. I would sit with him, talking, laughing, and reading, sometimes listening to music and dancing together. Sometimes, he'd be in his wheelchair, and sometimes on the floor. But always, when it came time for me to leave, he would pound his fists, flailing his whole body, and cling to me with his clenched hands, begging me to stay. I always assured him I'd be back tomorrow and tore myself away. The experience of getting to know him, spending time with him, and making a difference in his life stuck with me. Later, it became one of the compelling reasons for me to pursue my degree in teaching.

I did manage to make a few friends at work, but when you're constantly in survival mode, it changes who you are, how you think and feel. I didn't have the energy or confidence to be social. When you're constantly told you're worthless, criticized for everything you do, threatened, blamed for and accused of things you didn't do, belittled and put down day in and day out, it all takes a toll. Emotional abuse can be just as damaging as physical abuse, and I was suffering from both.

We had only been married a year, but in that time, I'd gone from being a somewhat confident, independent, outgoing, cheerful, self-sufficient person to someone who was withdrawn, sullen, depressed, and fearful. Even loud noises or people raising their voices around me was distressing. I was also ashamed of my situation. I had tried so many times throughout that year to explain it, to share it with others, and to seek advice or help from others and to break free of it, but every time I was met with dismissals, confusion, or an awkward discomfort. I had learned it was best to just keep it all to myself. Hiding the physical evidence of the abuse was harder. I wore long sleeves and pants in summer, and I used heavy makeup, sunglasses, or whatever I could to cover up the hard-to-explain bruises and marks.

When my mom visited me that summer from Seattle, she was horrified at my physical state. She hadn't seen me in the year since graduation and the wedding, and didn't know any of the details of what I'd been through. She'd been absorbed in her own divorce from my father and re-inventing her life. She had been a homemaker for the twenty years they were married and now was left holding an empty bag with no marketable skills or experience yet was expected to stand on her own two feet. Seeing the effect this had on her life would have a profound impact on me and later be the driving force behind my pursuit of a college degree.

She was shocked at how thin and gaunt I had become. I looked like maybe I'd had the flu for a few months. She threatened to take me to a hospital because I was so weak, severely underweight, had dark circles under my eyes, pale, splotchy skin, and no appetite. She could see that something was terribly wrong, but she didn't know what exactly. She only knew she was worried for me.

Despite her insistence, I refused, assuring her that, while I appreciated her concern, I was just tired and had been working too much. I didn't even have the energy to share with her all the details of my life and the abuse. Very soon I'd be grateful to her for this expression of concern, since it was one more seed planted, one that would eventually lead to the realization that I had to escape.

Part Three: The Big, Bad Wolf

Chapter 18

Beginning of the End

I REMEMBER IT LIKE it was yesterday, although it was forty years ago now...

The fear. The hopelessness. The desperation.

As I lay motionless on the rough, carpeted floor in the completely dark room, curled into a ball, trying to ignore the throbbing in my head and most of my body and trying to stay conscious, I waited for him to fall asleep while watching TV, as he often did. The carpet reeked of urine. It was all I could do to keep myself from vomiting. Larry often locked the dog in there for hours while he was gone, and the poor thing had had no choice but to pee on the carpet, knowing she'd be punished for it when her cruel master returned.

It was in those dark moments when I realized that escape was my only hope. I felt sure, if I didn't get away from him now, I was most definitely going to end up dead. I realized the irony of the fact that I had tried to end my own life only a short few weeks earlier. Now, my fuck-you gene was finally kicking in. It had seemed like I had lost it, but it had been there all along, buried deep in pain, suffering, and fear. I knew I certainly didn't want to die there on that stinky, nasty floor in that dark, cold room.

The words of my friend in Kansas who had tried to help me came back to me then, "*This isn't right. You need to get away from him.*" Another coworker had echoed those words just the week before, when she had asked about the bruises on my arms and my cut, swollen lip. I had bravely told her about how they got there, anticipating the usual reaction I received from people when they learned the truth. Most people immediately changed the subject, either because it made them uncomfortable, they didn't know what to say or do, or they felt that what went on behind closed doors was just none of their business.

She had *actually said*, "That's so wrong. You need to get away from that asshole."

Then there was also my mother's worry and insistence on taking me to a doctor, still fresh in my mind.

I decided I wanted to live, but first, I had to get free.

As soon as he falls asleep, I thought to myself, *I'll pull myself up and crawl out the window.* Even though the sill was about shoulder height and I was in terrible pain, I knew it was the only way out.

I knew our dog would hear me but she was so afraid of being hit for barking, she wouldn't dare. I hated to leave her behind, but I felt, if I didn't get out now, I may not have another chance, so I had to leave her.

His threats to kill me if I tried to leave no longer held power over me—I was pretty sure I was going to die anyway, so fuck it.

Part Three: The Big, Bad Wolf

On this particular night, I had come home after midnight because I had to stay late to help fill in for someone who hadn't shown up to work. When I walked through the door, I already knew what was coming. Larry was angry and started yelling at me about being late, accusing me of being out with another man.

I tried to explain that I had covered for another person who hadn't showed up for work, but that only made him madder. He insisted I was lying. He pushed me hard against the wall, banging my head, and smashed his fist into the wall next to my head, leaving a huge hole in the wall, (he'd left a long trail of holes in walls over the last year.) I ran for the bedroom and tried to close the door, but he pushed it in and backhanded me across the face. Coming from a man who was 6'5", this was a severe blow. It knocked my feet out from under me.

That was how I came to find myself on the floor, trying desperately to cover my gut and face though impossible, while the blows and kicks kept coming. Finally, his anger spent, he left me in a bloody, bruised heap, making a last remark over his shoulder as he left the room, "Fucking liar." Then he slammed the door behind him.

After waiting for what seemed like an eternity, I could hear his snoring and made my move. It took me a while to work the window open without making any noise and then a few attempts to pull myself up and out the window, not just because it was up so high, but also because of my injuries. I didn't have a watch, but I guessed it was sometime after 2 a.m. since I'd gotten off work at midnight.

It was pitch black, which for someone like me, who has night blindness, made it extra-challenging, but there were dim lights in the nearby parking lot, so I ran toward them. I continued down the street to the 7-Eleven, where I knew I could make a phone call. I asked the clerk if I could use their phone, since I had no money, although, fortunately I'd still had my purse in my hand when I'd run into the bedroom.

I called my friend, Keri, from my job at Pizza Hut. We had become friends and she knew a little about the beatings since there was often evidence that I couldn't hide. She'd said if I ever needed help, to call her. I took a chance, waiting breathlessly while the phone rang. She answered.

I had done the impossible—I got out. My fuck-you gene had finally kicked in. I dug down deep and found the strength to pull myself out of that hell hole, literally. But now what?

We had moved to Portland from Kansas, because he'd insisted that we move. A couple of years later, I learned that this was not only because it was his way of keeping me from leaving him, but it was also so he could escape from the large debt he had accrued in Kansas in only a year. So there I was, nineteen years old, in a town where I only had a couple of friends and no other support, trying to start over and build a new life for myself. No money, no car, no belongings. The one thing I did have, *my freedom.*

Going "home" wasn't an option, because for me there was no home to go to. My parents divorced shortly after I graduated high school, and since I'd been living on my own since sixteen, I didn't have a relationship with either of my parents. Certainly not the kind that would allow me to think I could turn to them now.

In my mind, they were part of the wolf pack of bullies and abusers that had plagued my life and what I needed now was to get away from the wolves, all of them. I needed a fresh start.

Part Three: The Big, Bad Wolf

Chapter 19

Do or Die

IT WAS THEN THAT I learned how to build a home within myself. I couldn't rely on anyone else to make me feel safe, to give me comfort, or to provide for my basic needs. I had to be self-sufficient and independent. *I was all I had.* Fortunately, everything I'd learned from my years of living as an army brat, moving every couple of years and watching my parents constantly readjust and acclimate to new homes, kicked in and allowed me to believe I was capable of rebuilding my life.

The dark cloud of fear, oppression, and suffering was lifted. I felt a sense of relief and lightness, and I even allowed myself to feel hopeful. I was riding the wave of pride that I had finally saved myself from what felt like certain death. Me. Lil' Red. I did it. No one else. I had a glimmer of self-assurance and self-worth that I hadn't experienced ever before. Maybe a little bit back when I was living in the camper outside my parents' apartment, but that was out of necessity – this was survival. I knew, deep down and without a doubt, no matter what he said or did, this time I would never go back.

Lil' Red

Again, from the outside it would seem the logical next step would have been to seek legal help and try to initiate a divorce. In my defense, I was in full survival mode and doing everything in my power to *hide* and make sure he couldn't find me or, worse, do as he'd promised so many times—come after me and kill me for leaving. I believed his threats. I knew he was capable of it. In his twisted mind, everything he did to me was justified. He had convinced me I didn't deserve freedom, happiness, or a life without him, that no one else would want me anyway. His mantra, "If he couldn't have me, no one could," echoed in my mind. So, the legal side of things would have to wait. For now, I just needed to be safe.

Fortunately, the same friend who answered my late-night call also offered me a place to stay. She was just moving to a new two-bedroom apartment and was looking for a roommate. *Perfect.* I moved in with her immediately, bringing along my garbage bag full of clothes that I had retrieved from the apartment when I knew he wouldn't be home. And, of course, my prized thirteen-inch black-and-white TV, as well as my treasured quilt. Larry had done me the favor of "purging" all my other belongings back in Kansas, when he smashed, burned, broke, and threw away practically everything I owned.

I rummaged around and found some old milk crates, cinder blocks, and wood to use as shelves and a wooden cable drum for a table, and I slept on the floor until someone at work was giving away an old bed. It wasn't much, but it was comfortable and I felt safe in that apartment. Moving so often while growing up taught me to live in the moment, not to look too far forward to the future. I was grateful for this moment of freedom and security—it was all I had. I was

Part Three: The Big, Bad Wolf

sure that the thirty-minute drive separating me from Larry was far enough away that he wouldn't find me.

I was wrong.

Of course, he knew where I worked, and within a couple of weeks, he started coming to Pizza Hut to harass me while I was working, saying over and over how I needed to come back to him. But not in a loving, pleading way. It was more of a demand than a request.

"Enough of this bullshit," he said. "Get your ass back where you belong."

One night, he waited for me to get off work then confronted me in the parking lot, threatening that if I didn't come back, he'd kill me. I didn't take the bus home that night. Instead, I went back inside the restaurant and hitched a ride home with a friend. After that, I asked a couple of the guys at work to escort me to the bus stop after closing, but they didn't want to get mixed up in it. Granted, Larry's size alone was intimidating, and when I told them about his threats to me, thinking this would convince them, they were almost as afraid of him as I was.

This went on for a couple of months. Then, one night, he managed to follow me home after work and found out where I lived. That was when I decided it was time to run again. The next day, I gathered up my meager belongings and found another apartment on my own using some money I'd saved from working my two jobs. I didn't need anything fancy. Just a small studio apartment in an old building was good enough.

I easily found a new job nearby as a hostess at a large-chain Mexican restaurant on the other side of town from Pizza Hut. My apartment was tiny, just one small room on the fourth floor that I again filled with my secondhand, pieced-together from trash furnishings to make it as homey and comfortable as I could. I felt safe again. I was sure there was no way he could find me now, so I began the task of rebuilding my life. Again.

I was happy at my new job. I made new friends with some of my coworkers and enjoyed lots of new experiences, the kind that normal nineteen-year-olds have. Some nights, a bunch of us would hop in someone's car after closing at 2 a.m. and drive the hour and a half to the coast to party on the beach until the sun came up. Sometimes, I was invited to a house party or maybe a hike to explore the mountains nearby. I even had a few romantic interests in those couple of months, which did wonders for my self-esteem. I started to forget my fear and fell into a rhythm of life that was positive, lighthearted, and free.

After a few months of this active new life, I arrived at work one afternoon and the manager pulled me aside and said, "There was a really tall guy who stopped by earlier, asking for you. Said he'd come back later."

My heart sank like a rock. I couldn't breathe. My eyes welled up with tears. Nervous, I looked around me and throughout the entire restaurant. I couldn't believe he'd found me again. It *had* to be him. Who else could it be? *But how?* I had still been in touch with a couple of my friends from Pizza Hut... maybe he charmed one of them into telling him where I was.

It didn't really matter how. All that mattered was that it was time for me to run again. I was used to this pattern from childhood—building a life, making connections, assimilating myself into a life, and then having to let it all go and restart. Maybe that's why it didn't phase me. I just matter-of-factly took the necessary steps and set about doing what I needed to do.

I quit my job, said my goodbyes, packed my things (clothes, a few personal items, my thirteen-inch black-and-white TV, and my quilt, of course), and moved on.

I knew, this time, I needed to move farther than just within Portland, so I decided to call my dad, to see if I might be able to go to Boise where he was living. I didn't tell him everything, just that I had left Larry and needed to get far enough away to feel safe, somewhere he couldn't find me.

I had saved a few hundred dollars, which I used to buy a 1971 Dodge Colt from a friend at work. It kind of resembled a bumble bee, bright yellow with a black stripe. It was cute, in an ugly kind of way. I didn't care. It was my first car, and it was *mine*.

My neighbor whom I had become friends with shared that he was moving to Colorado for work in a couple of weeks and offered to meet up with me there. I declined, saying that my dad had agreed to let me stay with him in Boise and I wanted to give that a try.

My fuck-you gene had kicked into overdrive now, and nothing was going to stop me.

Chapter 20

On the Run

THE SIX-HOUR DRIVE from Portland to Boise was so beautiful, it took me a full ten hours, because I kept stopping to enjoy the scenery. I'd been reminded of the effects of nature, how it calmed me and soothed my soul, during my midnight beach runs with friends and hikes on the Oregon Coast and in the mountains. Now, in my "new to me" car, on my way to the freedom and the safety of Idaho, nature was working its magic again. I felt strong, encouraged, and positive that this was the answer.

But these hopeful feelings were also mixed with worry about how it would all turn out. Surely *this* time, I was going far enough away, I told myself. He would never *think* to look for me there.

When I arrived in Boise, anticipating that I was going to be staying with my dad, he informed me that, actually, he didn't have room for me, but he said I was welcome to stay with my grandmother. After the divorce from my mother, he had remarried. My guess was the new wife didn't want me around.

Part Three: The Big, Bad Wolf

I was extremely disappointed and hurt. Here I was in this desperate situation, running for my life from my abuser and looking to him for comfort, consolation, and sympathy, and instead, he was passing me off on my grandmother.

As it seemed I had no other choice, I agreed and moved into a small room in my grandma's double-wide trailer. I admit, prior to this, what little knowledge or opinion I had of trailer parks was pretty low. To my surprise, I found my grandma's park to be very clean and well-maintained. All the homes had small yards with carefully manicured gardens. It was so tranquil and beautiful, it actually lifted my spirits and gave me a sense of hope that maybe this was all going to work out after all.

I readily found a job at a local burger place and began trying to build a life for myself there. I was getting good at this starting-over thing. I enjoyed connecting with my red-headed cousin, too. We were close in age, so we had fun going out to bars or hanging with her and her friends. In Idaho, I was legally allowed to go to the bars, since the age limit was nineteen and I had just turned twenty. In fact, my cousin and I looked enough alike that I was able to lend her my ID to get her into the bars, too, even though she was only eighteen.

I even enjoyed my time with my grandma, to my surprise, although I quickly found out she wanted to exert more power and control over my lifestyle than I felt was appropriate. She didn't agree with my going out to bars, legal or not, or staying out late, or the way I dressed, which wasn't particularly slutty but anything less than matronly was inappropriate in her eyes. We had regular intense arguments over those issues, mixed with quiet nights of sitting together watching TV, doing puzzles, or enjoying stories of our family's history.

During my first two months in Boise, I only saw my dad twice, which I found incredibly frustrating and disappointing. Several years later, I came to understand that this was due to his own struggles with his new wife, as well as trying to reinvent himself and start a new career after his recent retirement from a twenty-year career in the military. Ultimately, even though I was having some lifestyle clashes with my grandmother, with her traditional religious culture at the center, I felt like we were managing all right and I was actually enjoying it.

That is until one afternoon in early summer, when my dad called and asked if I could come meet him over at the church. This seemed strange after not being in touch with him that much since I'd arrived, but he said he had something important to discuss with me, so I agreed. As I drove there, I had an uneasy, heavy feeling in my gut. When I rounded the corner and entered the parking lot, I realized why. There, standing next to my father, was Larry.

I'll never forget the depth of the betrayal I felt at that moment.

Larry had somehow tracked down my dad through my grandmother and convinced him that he deserved a chance at reconciliation. In my dad's defense, he didn't know about the many chances I'd already given him and how many times I had tried to get away, only to be convinced to return. He did know I had left Portland after a couple of failed attempts to get away from Larry. I had also told him I was afraid of him. But my dad didn't know the full extent of the abuse I'd suffered or any of the details.

Part Three: The Big, Bad Wolf

His extremely conservative religious convictions played a big part in his decision to disclose my location to Larry. My dad felt it was his duty to try to mediate. In the eyes of the church, and my father, I had made a lifetime commitment, for better or worse and I was supposed to do everything I could to see it through.

I saw things differently, of course. In my mind, the person I had trusted to help keep me safe had just betrayed me to the man who had caused me so much pain. I looked at my father and said, "How could you? I trusted you." I turned my back on both of them and walked away.

I didn't even give Larry the chance to spew his bullshit. I'd heard his hollow promises, apologies and excuses so many times before, I could recite them verbatim. If it wasn't that, it was threats. I didn't want to hear either.

With my fuck-you gene in my pocket, I got back in my car without another word and drove straight back to my grandmother's, where I quickly packed my belongings (I was really good at this by now). I said my goodbyes to her, thanked her for giving me a place to stay, and began the twenty-one-hour drive to Colorado.

This time, I didn't tell *anyone* where I was going.

Chapter 21

Finally Free

I ARRIVED IN COLORADO during a horrific summer rainstorm, exhausted after twenty-one hours of driving straight through. It was so bad, it flooded a portion of I-25, the main highway through Denver, causing it to close and me to be diverted. The directions I had to my friend's apartment were from I-25, but I found myself on some other road in a torrential downpour. Frustrated and lost, I decided to pull over and park in a gas station until the rain subsided. I succumbed to the overwhelming mental and physical exhaustion and, despite the discomfort of sitting upright in my car, fell fast asleep.

A few hours later, I awoke to clear skies, found my way back onto the highway, and managed to find my friend's place. He kindly offered to let me stay there until I could find a job and a place to live.

The same skimpy outfit that had landed me the aerobics-instructor job in Portland also got me a cocktail waitress job in Colorado the very next day. It was for the same chain Mexican restaurant I had worked for in Portland, but this one felt different. For starters, it was much

Part Three: The Big, Bad Wolf

bigger and busier. It was also in a rough part of town, which meant the police were called every weekend because of the fights that broke out consistently. That would eventually lead to the demise of the bar.

Although I wasn't twenty-one yet, the legal drinking age in Colorado, I attributed the fact that I was hired to serve cocktails to the simple fact that I looked good in the skimpy outfit. When I worked the crazy-busy nights, Thursday through Saturday, it was so crowded I had to walk, scantily clad, through the mobs of customers with a full tray of drinks up over my head, getting groped and rubbed against the whole night. It was worth it, though, as I made $200-300 a night in tips, and I desperately needed the money.

While I was saving to get my own place, I enjoyed the comfort, safety, and companionship of my friend's apartment. It was good to feel safe again. I was so grateful for his generosity and kindness.

After a few short months, the bar closed and I found a new job as a receptionist in an office, my first "real" job, where I got a steady paycheck. I didn't really care for it, but I worked with some fun people and the position had some great perks, like driving the boss's black Porsche 944 to run his errands. I moved into a house one of my coworkers was looking after for a friend, but that only lasted a few months as I quickly realized we had very different ideas about cleanliness and lifestyles.

I decided I wanted to go to college, so I moved up to Boulder near the University of Colorado. I had a small, overpriced studio apartment, complete with a Murphy bed and roaches. Colorado doesn't have roaches. These were imported by students who brought them in with their belongings from other states. I was used to living with them from my time in Kansas, so I just adapted and got used to sleeping with the lights on.

By this time, I felt certain I had finally gotten far enough away from Larry and that he wasn't coming after me. He had roots in Oregon, and I was pretty sure he wasn't coming all the way to Colorado, nor would he have *any* reason to look for me there. After a recommendation from someone I knew, I reached out to the safehouse for battered women near me and they encouraged me to pursue legal options for finalizing my freedom from him. It was the last step, and although it meant disclosing my location to him, I knew it was the only way to really be completely free.

Reaching out to the safehouse was one of the smartest things I did. Safehouses for battered women are shelters created to offer victims of domestic violence a safe haven. Most victims are faced with many obstacles that prevent them from leaving a violent situation, with not having a safe place to go leading the pack. There's also a lack of finances, fear for their lives, lack of belief in themselves, shame, and usually lack of support due to the isolation commonly created by abusers. Safehouses offer housing in crisis situations providing for basic needs while a victim is figuring out the next steps. They offer legal and medical support, emotional and educational support, and may even escort victims to police stations or court.

I didn't personally need housing support, but I did join their outreach group counseling, utilized their extensive resources, and found the validation and affirmation I had been searching for. *Finally*, someone heard me. They not only validated my fears, pain, and suffering, but they

Part Three: The Big, Bad Wolf

offered support for how to begin the long journey of healing from the abuse I had suffered.

In the group therapy sessions, I heard the stories of so many other women that were similar to mine. Some were even much worse, which made me grateful I had gotten out when I did. There were women who had been with their abusers for five, ten, even twenty years or more. They had endured unspeakable acts of violence. One woman was covered in scars all over her arms and legs, even her neck, from the repeated cigarette burns her husband inflicted. Another didn't have the use of one arm, because her husband had broken it so many times. There was even a woman who had scarring on her face and neck from the boiling hot water her husband threw on her.

All the things I had suffered at the hands of my husband didn't even begin to compare to what these women had been through. I knew, if they could survive, escape their abusers, and have hope for rebuilding their lives, then I could, too. They inspired me to push on. We cried together, unburdened our souls to one another, and worked together to overcome the many challenges we faced on our journey to healing and building our new lives.

With help from the legal aid provided through the safehouse, I filed for divorce and officially gave Larry notice. I waited anxiously for the signed papers to be returned to me, hoping they would arrive by mail rather than him showing up at my doorstep again.

It also meant I had to accept responsibility for half of the debt he had accrued while we were in Kansas, which I did reluctantly. I'd worked so hard that year and half living with him, at two jobs even while pregnant, and he'd just wasted our money on junk cars and other stuff, most of which he'd sold when we left there. But what could I do? It was part of the cost of freedom.

A few weeks later, that long-awaited day came. I received the signed papers. I was legally *free*. It took a while to sink in that he was actually letting me go, but when it did, it felt good. I could breathe deeply again and stop looking over my shoulder all the time.

Now that I was legally divorced, with a new job and safely established in my new home, I continued to focus on my healing journey. I volunteered at the safehouse in the capacity of a Victim's Advocate, someone who is called, usually in the middle of the night, to the scene of a domestic violence disturbance by the police, to console and advise the victim. Using my own painful experiences as fuel to help other victims had a profound impact on me. It helped me process my pain, moving it from the forefront to another part of me where it was still there but not affecting my responses to everyday events. I had shifted out of survival mode and into a new rhythm of life.

I continued my work with victims of domestic abuse by creating a "Clothing Closet" housed on-site at the safehouse in Boulder. Most victims leave their abusers in crisis mode, often with nothing more than the clothes on their backs. They are usually faced with the challenge of needing to find work and establish financial independence. The safehouse offered extensive counseling and support as well as educational opportunities to help victims navigate this extremely difficult endeavor. That was where I came in.

I would meet with the client one-on-one to walk them through the closet and help them put together outfits appropriate for the job interviews they were seeking that were flattering for their body type and fit well. I stocked the

Part Three: The Big, Bad Wolf

closet with clothes I found at garage sales and thrift shops, or through donations from people in the community. Helping other victims regain their confidence and being a part of providing for their basic needs on their journey to freedom and independence was empowering, for them and for me. I continued providing this service for several years before passing it on to someone else to manage.

While the volunteering efforts proved to be instrumental in my healing, I also felt it was beneficial to attend the group sessions through the outreach center. I made progress through one-on-one counseling sessions on rebuilding my self-worth and regaining my strength and my belief in myself. My individual counselor helped me recognize the other effects the abuse had on me. She helped me rebuild trust in others, to realize that the abuse wasn't my fault, and taught me how to deal with the painful memories. She encouraged me to talk about it, to continue sharing in the group therapy, and to express the past pain and trauma with those close to me.

I also continued to seek out nature as a form of therapy. It was something I could turn to at any time, and it always gave me the peace, comfort, and solace I needed. I learned that rather than succumbing to the temptation and my natural inclination to seek distractions and gloss over the pain and push it down, the best way to deal with it was to acknowledge it, face it, feel it, let it out, and go all the way through it.

While all of this internal "house cleaning" was productive, it was really only dealing with the current trauma caused by Larry. There were still plenty of scars from my childhood traumas that needed healing, but that would come later. I believe we are not our pains and sorrows of the past, that they don't have to define us. But we do bear those scars left behind to remind us of that pain so we can know how much we've grown, how strong we've become, and what we've had to overcome to be who we are.

All my healing and growth was forging a new me, a stronger, more resilient me. An independent and self-sufficient me capable of anything I set my mind to. A version of me who would not only believe in herself but share her experience and knowledge with others to encourage them to live their best lives as well. It was my turn to be the wolf, the kind that is strong, determined, resilient and courageous.

A She-Wolf.

PART FOUR
The She-Wolf

She-Wolf: One who possesses great determination, strength, endurance, and survival skills, supported by highly developed senses; fiercely loyal with strong family connections; one who is resilient, powerful, and most of all... brave.

She trusts her intuition and has the courage to initiate change, in herself and others.

She is not fearless, but she's not afraid of trying.

She is a force to be reckoned with.

Lil' Red

Part Four: The She-Wolf

Chapter 22

Her Spirit

RESILIENCE IS THE CAPACITY to withstand or to recover from adversity; strength of character, toughness.

I think resilience is something we choose, something we can learn. I also think we all have it within us, that we *choose* to tap into it, we *choose* to develop it, and we *choose* to engage it when we need it.

I believe resilience is something that can be passed down from one generation to the next, right alongside pain and trauma. My great-grandmother, Gammy, had grit, she was tough. She had to have been, in order to survive moving west in a covered wagon as a girl and to live through all that the world threw her way during her eighty-five years on this earth.

My mother, Darlene, endured so much adversity in life, from the challenges of her family life to surviving abuse to raising three young children so close in age under less-than-ideal circumstances. She was able to move herself forward in search of a better life and then did everything in her power to build and maintain it.

Just as the pain and trauma they both endured was passed along to me through their genes, so was their ability to overcome hardship. They unknowingly passed on the weight of the burdens they bore, but they also passed along their resilience. I, too, have unintentionally passed on some of my past trauma to my own daughters through my genes, but I most definitely, consciously gave them the skills and knowledge to learn from, adapt to, and recover from hardships and adversity. They may not have inherited my red hair, but I know I passed on my fuck-you gene and the fighting Irish spirit that goes with it. Some of us may have more resilience from birth than others, but if you happen to be one of those who didn't have it passed on to you, you can absolutely learn how to develop it, grow it, nurture it, and tap into it.

Resilience takes many forms. It's someone who knows their feelings and needs and who looks at hardships and adversity as opportunities for learning and growth. It can be someone who sees opportunities for change and improvement and takes action, someone who makes things happen. It's someone who takes care of themselves, who prioritizes their health and well-being, and who connects with others and seeks support.

The most critical part of resilience is fortification. We've got to fortify ourselves, build ourselves up, nourish our mind, body and soul, so we're ready for the times when we need to call on our resilience.

I didn't know what it was called back then, but I figured out, as a young girl that creating a safe, comfortable space for myself, was a form of resilience. It was a way for me to protect and insulate myself, a way of creating a place to

Part Four: The She-Wolf

retreat and recover from the bullying and abuse I was experiencing.

Later, as a young adult, I created a refuge for myself, a safe space, as well as a place for reflection and contemplation. Throughout my adult life, creating a welcoming, uplifting space for myself and family allowed us to practice resilience by giving us a home base that provided a calm, safe place for each of us to recharge and reset our mind, body, and soul. The importance of creating this space for ourselves cannot be underrated.

A big part of creating that calm space is removing clutter. Just as much as we need to declutter our heart and soul emotionally, we need to declutter our physical space, as well. Decluttering reduces stress and anxiety and can increase your focus, productivity, and creativity.

When I chose to leave my abusive marriage, I had to call on my resilience, as well as every bit of strength, determination, and resolve I could muster. Whenever I refer to that time in my life, I like to say that my fuck-you gene finally kicked in, because that's how it felt. Like the life was being sucked out of me—or, more accurately, beaten out of me—and I finally said, *"Enough. Fuck you."*

When, at fourteen, I grabbed my mother's hand with a belt in it and said, *"No more. Fuck you."* Even when I lashed out at the bullies in school, although admittedly there was a better way and I just didn't know it, I was saying, *"Stop! Fuck you."*

I was in my early forties when my friend, Christine, coined this phrase, "the fuck-you gene," and I realized I had it in spades. I *had* resilience, determination, tenacity, grit, resolve, strength of character—I had all those qualities,

Lil' Red

because I had *chosen* to dig down deep and call them up. Then, I developed, practiced, and cultivated them.

Some of us have the fuck-you gene, and some of us are born doers. Maybe there's a connection because they're both about belief in ourselves, that we can do *anything*. I recently had my DNA analysis done and was told I have a gene that explains why I have so much energy, so there's apparently a genetic element that contributes to my ability to get things done. This makes sense. I've always known that my brain seems to be in high gear a lot of the time. Even if I'm sitting still, watching a movie or something on TV, for example, I'm usually doing something else at the same time. I just have an overly active brain. Over the years, I've learned to tap into that energy and make the most of it.

I've noticed that one of the differences I see between myself and people around me is that they often think of the same things I do, they have an idea for something fun to do, to create, something to build or learn, but then that's it. They forget about it or get busy with other things. They overanalyze and overthink it to the point of inaction. Or sometimes they just assume they couldn't possibly do *that*, whatever that is.

The difference between us is that I *do the thing*. I go on Google or YouTube, or ask someone with more knowledge and experience, and figure out how to build or do the thing. I carve out time and get it done. I organize a fun event, a dinner with friends, or a cool trip somewhere. I built those stilts with my neighbor, Billy when I was eight. I built the fort in the garage. I climbed the rock wall when I was five. I got my college degree even though it took ten years. I learned about interior design and used that knowledge to remodel many homes over the years, and also design a

Part Four: The She-Wolf

small boutique hotel and bar/restaurant in Mexico. I realized my fear of water was irrational and in my late forties, finally conquered it. I'm that person who stops what I'm doing and orders the cool gadget I see advertised or that someone tells me about. I go and try the new restaurant, hike a new trail, paddleboard a new spot. I renovate my house or redesign a room. You get the idea – I'm a do-er, I get things done.

So much so that, when I was in my early forties, I officially appointed myself the "Ambassador of Fun." I found I was always the one bringing friends together and organizing social activities or trips, book clubs, or my home repair club. I was facilitating the fun that others thought about doing and wanted to do, but *I* was the one making things happen. A big part of being a doer is believing that you can, ignoring those thoughts of self-doubt, and pushing through, finding a way to get it done. Sometimes this "I can do anything" attitude gets me into trouble, I get in over my head. But mostly it just gets me to a place where I have amazing experiences in life that I wouldn't have had otherwise and that others only dream of.

I look back at my life as a full-time mom and am in awe of my energy and enthusiasm for life during those years. I seemed to have endless energy for DIY home-improvement projects, sewing clothes and costumes for my girls (like my mother did), cooking, baking elaborate birthday cakes, and throwing themed birthday parties, all while getting my bachelor's degree, engaging in social activities with friends, and volunteering at my daughters' school or in the community. And somehow, I still managed to get several hours' sleep each night! I'm not really sure how I did it all those years—I didn't even drink coffee at the time! I like to think of it as just me getting the most out of life, my way of living. My Reditude! I continually make it a point to look back, reflect on and draw from that energy in my present life.

Those years, the twenty or so years while I was raising my daughters, weren't without hardship and adversity, though. I had to continually fortify myself and call on my resilience many times. Fortification is such an important part of resilience. We have to build up our reserves, mentally, physically, and emotionally, so that, when the time comes to call on our resilience, it's there, ready for action. We do that through self-care, loving ourselves and being kind, patient, and forgiving to ourselves and others.

Another key element of resilience is emotional purging. When we bravely cleanse our souls of past pain and trauma, when we go all the way through it and come out the other side of it, we make room for contentment, peace, and calmness. I call it "clearing out the emotional clutter."

For me, this cleansing came in waves, first with the group therapy in the outreach program at the safehouse, then through volunteering and helping others, and then through forgiveness for all the Little Wolves, the Mama and Papa Wolves, and the Big Bad Wolf in my life. None of these journeys were easy, each one took time. I had to allow myself time and space to grieve, time to reflect, and then open my heart to be sympathetic, empathetic, and understanding.

Writing this book was another choice that allowed me to delve more deeply into my past pain and suffering. Through writing, I've explored my past more than ever before. In the process, I've learned new things about myself, uncovered many more good memories from childhood, and

Part Four: The She-Wolf

have so many new things to be grateful for. I also uncovered some dark corners that still needed purging, a little bit of emotional clutter. Taking this deep dive has been incredibly therapeutic and cathartic, something I'd highly recommend to anyone, even if it's in the form of journaling and only for yourself.

A good friend, Raina O'Dell, an accomplished author and inspirational life coach, turned me on to the idea of focusing on constructing your life based on how you want your life to *feel*. It's important to seek out the things that bring us joy and focus on the *feeling* we get from the life we create for ourselves.

I've found that spending time in nature has always been grounding. It provides a feeling of serenity, calmness, and peace that refreshes and invigorates me. I often find it gives me the opportunity for self-reflection, self-examination, and contemplation. Especially being near water, whether it's a river, lake, or ocean.

For me, being near water feels especially soothing, which is pretty incredible considering I was so deathly afraid of water, of being *in* it or *on* it, until about ten years ago when I decided to get over my fear. I've sought out water whether it was the lake we lived next to at my last home in Colorado, or on the Gulf of Mexico where I live now.

Now that I'm living my dream life on the beach, I am grateful to spend time each day feeling my toes in the sand and listening to the sound of the waves that lull me to sleep every night. The trick is making time for it and prioritizing it, whatever *it* is for you. It's so easy to get swallowed up in the "busyness" of life, so easy to lose track of the things that matter. Especially when we've got things like the many streaming services on television plus social media and a million other things vying for our attention.

It's worthwhile to take time to acknowledge our strengths and weaknesses (our humanity), our growth and victories, big and small. We've got to regularly congratulate and celebrate ourselves. For me, after having had low self-worth (my internal sense of value) and poor self-esteem (my level of confidence in that value) throughout most of my life, I have learned to build myself up a little at a time. Celebrating my continual growth and successes, no matter how small, goes a long way toward building that foundation. Undoing the damage that was done by the wolves in my early life has taken many, many years of concentrated effort.

Having my three incredible daughters has also been a tremendous help in rebuilding my self-worth. I decided, when they were young, I wanted to nurture and shape them to be strong, confident women. I was determined they would not experience the low self-esteem that I had, growing up. I worked hard to instill that confidence, self-reliance, and belief in themselves, and in doing so, I realized the best way to do it was to serve as an example for them. Surrounding myself with loving and supportive family and friends, who also build me up and encourage me to be my best self, living my best life, has made all the difference in the world.

Something incredibly valuable I learned after my second divorce was about how to allow room for my own humanity. It's so much healthier if we just admit we're only human, even if others expect something different from us. This means we accept that we have character flaws we need to acknowledge and own up to. It gives us permission to improve on them, too, without criticism or judgment from ourselves or others. We can even bring a sense of humor to it, a teasing, playful lightness. Sometimes, I joke with my husband that my "impatience is showing." Or when I get irritable, we call it feeling "prickly." It's our way of acknowledging and allowing for my humanity. When we give ourselves room to be human, we have the freedom to make mistakes and learn from them, to make adjustments in our lives, and even to try new things without fear.

This honesty in owning our flaws also helps us see that the flip side of them is always a positive, a strength. I tend to have a lack of patience, but the positive side of that is that I'm also very decisive. I know what I want and when I set my mind to something, it gets done. I also have a bit of a temper (I get to blame *that* on the red hair!), but the flip side is I am very good at expressing myself, and you always know where you stand with me. I'm also not afraid to assert myself and rarely shy away from confrontation.

Knowing our flaws and acknowledging the other side of them helps us fortify ourselves, build ourselves up. And when we've thoroughly fortified ourselves, we are prepared for the hardships that life throws at us. We can call on that fuck-you gene and say, *"I've got this. I'm ready to grow and learn from this. I can survive this."* The more we do it, practice it, and grow it, the better at living a resilient life we get.

Fortification also requires determination, and determination will get you *everywhere.*

No one is going to do it for you.

No one is going to design your best life and hand it to you.
You have to decide what you need and go get it.
You have to show up and do the work.
You have to be determined and committed to living your best life.

But not all at once! And you don't have to do it alone. I think, oftentimes we get overwhelmed when it seems like there are just too many things we want to change in our lives. Instead, we freeze up and shut down, taking no action at all.

Sometimes we find what we need within ourselves, and sometimes we need inspiration, guidance, and assistance from someone else. Remember the saying, "It takes a village"? It's okay to let others help us on our journey. Let them support you, let them share their knowledge and experience with you, and let them help you. Read books, do research, listen to podcasts, hire a life coach, see a therapist, or reach out to trusted friends or family.

You also don't have to change everything all at once. You're better off choosing *one* thing at a time and then do *a little less of this and a little more of that* each day. Take baby steps toward your goal and work your way up to a life full of moments that feed your soul.

I recently decided I wanted to spend more time exercising, so I started doing a little less time scrolling social media and a little more time exercising. It was a matter of taking an honest look at how I was spending my time, choosing what thing to prioritize, and then making *small shifts* each day toward my goal. These small, gradual changes and improvements are what build and fortify us.

Part Four: The She-Wolf

An important part of growth is the celebration of it. It's funny, how we're often so quick to judge, condemn, or berate ourselves, when we take missteps, but slow to celebrate the victories over past traumas, to celebrate strength and resilience, to celebrate the small changes.

Take time to reap the fruits of the labor of love that is fortifying yourself.

Once you've cleaned out your emotional closet, purged emotionally and physically, focused on creating a fulfilling, fortified life surrounded by family and friends, your pack, and armed yourself with Reditude and some fuck-you gene, you'll be ready for anything!

You, too, will *BE* the She-Wolf.

Chapter 23

Her Den

THROUGHOUT MY LIFE, an essential part of my fortification has been to create comfortable, inviting, safe spaces for myself. It began when I was as young as four or five years old, when I built "forts" with my sister and brother out of blankets and sheets draped over furniture or that fort with my friend, Billy, in the rafters of our garage. We piled lots of pillows inside and curled up with books, toys, or even snacks, enjoying the comfort of our temporary haven.

Whenever I was at my great-grandparents' home, I found comfort in their back garden, especially on the porch swing, among the apple trees, or cozied up with my siblings in their attic. During the time we lived in Maryland, I found solace in the forest behind our house most days. While there, I would often build a kind of room for myself using branches and leaves.

For many years, I enjoyed the refuge of my shared bedroom with my sister. I loved our room not just because it afforded me the intimate, one-on-one time with her that I

Part Four: The She-Wolf

valued, but also because I loved the way it felt—colorful, cozy, and inviting.

We each had our own twin canopy bed, with a brightly colored, patterned quilt and canopy to match. Our grandmother made us quilts that coordinated with the bedding our mother purchased from Sears. I was in awe of the intricate little triangles and squares, which she had so carefully pieced together, knowing how much time and effort must have gone into making it. This quilt was a lifeline for me, to the family that was so distant, and I clung to it like it was life itself.

Our "suite" of furniture from Sears included a matching dresser and nightstands that were off-white with gold accents and eloquently curved edges. I treasure the memories of time spent in that room with my sister, playing, giggling, and talking, along with the closeness we shared.

When we moved to Germany, my sister and I had separate rooms which was a huge adjustment for me, initially. It took me a while, but I came around to enjoying my privacy and being able to decorate my own room the way I wanted to. This meant more cows, of course. Instead of bands or TV stars, I had cow posters. Cow knickknacks. The more cows the better. The crown jewel was a bright lime-green carpet I'd convinced my mom to get for me. It was army housing, which meant we couldn't paint, but the carpet covered most of my room and gave the effect I was looking for. Since it was so bright, a bold choice for sure, it had a huge impact and made its own statement.

I felt happy there and spent a lot of time in my room, playing, daydreaming, or reading my *Nancy Drew Mystery* novels or my favorite book, *Charlie and the Chocolate Factory*,

Lil' Red

over and over. During those couple of years in Germany, I continued to find comfort in nature, spending afternoons on my own in the park behind our house. I played softball on the field, but I also liked to go there by myself and just hang out, maybe smoke a cigarette and have a good think. I was in my "tweens," experiencing lots of transitions, physical and emotional, so I had *a lot* to think about.

My mother also enjoyed decorating. Each time we moved, she created a new, comfortable space for us, often using bold colors. When I was very young, we had a turquoise-blue, brocade couch. And when I was a teen, we had a dark-rust, tufted-velvet couch. It sounds tacky, but she did a good job of putting things together to make it all cohesive and tasteful.

While we lived in Germany, she took advantage of being in Europe and having access to unique furnishings. As we traveled around Europe, something I'm forever grateful to my parents for doing with us, she acquired things like a marble chess table with elaborately carved chairs, some original oil paintings, a large, carved wooden screen, a beautiful grandfather clock, a carved wood cuckoo clock, and other decorative items. Whether it was an outlet for pent-up frustrations or just because she enjoyed doing it, I'm not sure, but she often rearranged our living room, seemingly on a whim. I liked this about her. I think my interest in interior design and some of my natural creative abilities came from her and the influence of how she decorated.

After Germany, we moved back to Washington State, where I lived until I finished high school. I remember, when we first arrived, we were staying as a family in the BOQ housing (temporary housing for officers), and my dad

Part Four: The She-Wolf

immediately recognized that having two teenage girls on an army base full of young soldiers was *not* a good combination. We were getting way too much attention. We quickly found a house off base and settled in there. The problem for me was that I was expected to share a room with my younger brother.

At that time, we were thirteen and twelve years old respectively. For obvious reasons, puberty being the main one, this wasn't anything like sharing with my sister, and I was adamantly against it. I petitioned my mom to let me make a room for myself in the small storage room off the back of the garage. It was just big enough for a twin bed, a side table, and a chest of drawers, which I put at the end of the bed to serve as a kind of wall for privacy. I even put up a couple of posters on the back side of it, to make it feel more wall-like. It wasn't ideal, but I made it work by surrounding myself with stuffed animals, pillows I'd made on my mom's sewing machine, and my grandmother's special quilt.

The other place where I found solitude in that house was the coat closet. I know, it sounds ridiculous but hear me out. My dad had some high-quality Pioneer-brand stereo equipment that he put on the shelves at the back of that closet, including a pair of headphones. I would take some pillows, pile them in front of the shelves, put the headphones on and sit in there for hours listening to his records. This also meant I had a kind of weird taste in music for someone my age, his choices not mine, including Roger Whittaker, Herb Albert, the Carpenters, and the Mamas and the Papas, but it was my way to escape, so I made it work.

Over the first year of my first marriage, when we lived in Kansas, I had no escape, no safe place, no harbor where I could get away from the violence. I was so busy working to support us, I didn't even have time to get out and enjoy the comfort of nature. It wasn't until we were in Portland and I finally got away from him that I was able to create my own sanctuary again. This was where I really learned the lesson that it doesn't take money to create an inviting, comfortable, soothing space.

I didn't even have a bed. But I had blankets and pillows, including my special quilt, all of which I piled along the wall and in the corner to make it cozier. I had a milk crate side table, where I set my little thirteen-inch black-and-white TV. I also put up a few posters I found at a yard sale for fifty cents each. Even though it was a little lacking in physical comfort, the fact that I wasn't living in fear of being hit, kicked, threatened, or yelled at every day instantly made it feel ten-times more safe and comforting.

I also enjoyed a deep connection with nature during my time in Oregon, hiking in the mountains with friends or enjoying short visits to the beach. I was still deathly afraid of water at that time, since I didn't know how to swim and hadn't spent much time around water growing up. I continued to seek it out throughout my life though, whether a river, creek, or lake, or ocean and felt that being near water provided much-needed solitude, healing, rejuvenation, and time for contemplation. I decided during that time that, someday, I would live on the beach.

Although I was on the run for the next couple of years, with barely enough income to provide the basics for myself, I continued to recreate this same retreat in each new place I landed. I also spent as much time as possible in nature, hiking or just walking through a park or sitting by a pond or river.

Part Four: The She-Wolf

Throughout my life, I've continued to use this skill for making a safe, comfortable, welcoming space not just for myself, but for my family and friends, too. It's a passion of mine to help provide the same feeling of comfort, solace, warmth, and coziness for others. I believe our homes are our sanctuaries, a place to escape the world and retreat to safety. They should be places that always welcome us back, wrapping us up in comfort.

I realize this need for a safe, comforting shelter comes from living in so many different places as a child, as well as the deep rejection I felt when my parents moved to homes where there wasn't a place for me. First, when we moved to the house in Washington and I was expected to share a room with my teenage brother. Second, when they later moved to the apartment where I was again somehow expected to share a room with him at age sixteen. I felt like I was an afterthought, like I hadn't been considered at all when they chose that home. In fact, it went beyond that. There had already been conversations during the year leading up to that move and threats to send me away to my grandmother in Idaho, so moving to a place with no room for me solidified my feeling that I was unwanted. This had a deep and long-lasting effect on me. It permanently altered something inside of me.

My need to create a place for myself in the world showed itself in many ways later in life. As an adult, when I was married to my daughters' father, I insisted we live within the same town during their school years. Although we lived in three different houses within that town over those years, I desperately wanted to provide them with the stability of growing up in one place, where you knew the kids you went to school with and had friends for many years.

Of course, the challenge with this philosophy is that our children could have ended up with a limited, skewed view of the world. But since we were aware of that, we made it a point to travel extensively as a family, providing them with a broader world view. I felt that staying in one place and having a solid home foundation was grounding, and this was critical for my kids as it was something I never had. Even though we never had extended family living nearby in Colorado, we always made it a point to stay connected to and visit family over the years, as well. Our kids also benefited from the close circle of friends, our "chosen" family, in their hometown.

Much later in life, I became aware that my feeling unwanted as a child meant that I was also overly sensitive to being included, whether it was having a seat saved for me at a restaurant when a group of friends gathered or playing a game during a family social gathering or just being included in a conversation. It mattered deeply to me. After several instances of overreaction on my part, creating unnecessary conflict and over-dramatizing, I took a step back to evaluate the reasons behind those reactions.

Once I finally realized these feelings were connected to my childhood experiences, I could address that pain and trauma, learn from it, and move forward. I was able to better explain myself to those around me, alerting them to my oversensitivity. Acknowledging those influences from my past also allowed me to adjust within my own mind and lessen my reaction by doing some self-talk.

When I find myself in situations where I feel left out but know other people aren't doing it intentionally, I stop

Part Four: The She-Wolf

myself, count to ten, remind myself that I'm not Lil' Red anymore, and just voice my desire to be included. Or I go grab my own chair and join in, sometimes even making a joke of it, "Hey guys! You forgot about me!" Or I sit on someone's lap! You get the idea. Lighten the mood, steer away from the drama and conflict, and assume there are no bad intentions or malice. You hear people say, don't dwell in the past. However, in this case, looking into my past provided me with a chance for some healing, learning, and growth, which was valuable for the present and future.

My need to create comfortable, safe spaces for myself is something I turned into a passion. I don't practice interior design for a living, but it gives me great joy to be able to impact others' lives by giving them the gift of comfort and enjoyment in their personal spaces. Back in my twenties, I started learning about design and DIY through watching television programs like the ones on HGTV. I'm not saying I learned to save lives by watching *ER* on TV (yes, I know someone who actually said that once!), but I did learn a lot from watching, doing and a great deal of trial and error. I found I had a natural instinct for it, as well. I also read books about design, observed and analyzed it around me wherever I went, and even took a few courses at one point, when I thought I might make a career out of it.

My favorite pastime was finding secondhand furniture, often items no one else wanted and maybe even thrown away, and transforming them into beautiful pieces I could use to decorate my home. This was partially because we didn't have much disposable income at the time and couldn't afford expensive things. But it was more because I just enjoyed doing it. I also did all the painting myself, sewed curtains or pillows, and even reupholstered an old chair I'd found on the curbside. I was putting into practice the same principle I learned when I was younger about creating something from nothing, using what you have and putting in some "elbow grease" to create a beautiful, comfortable, inviting space.

Over the years, I've enjoyed decorating and remodeling our family homes. When I divorced for the second time, I found myself in the position of owning my first home all my own. I enjoyed the deep dive of completely gutting and renovating it. It was the first time I was able to make all the decisions myself, so I splurged on every little detail and went all out. I was wise to choose an amazing team of experts to support me, from the architect to the contractor and interior designer. Our "Dream Team" I called it. Together we created an incredible space that ended up being in *Luxe Magazine,* which to this day is one of my crowning achievements, something I'm incredibly proud of.

Another major project and point of pride for me was designing the interior of a ten-room hotel in Mexico. My dear friend is an incredibly talented architect with whom I had worked on a couple of home renovations in Mexico. I appreciated that, even though I didn't have formal training or certification as a designer, he trusted me implicitly with the hotel project. Aside from input on the budget and the overall style, he gave me complete autonomy. It was the biggest design project I'd ever done. It took about a year to complete, but it turned out incredibly well and was deeply satisfying.

That same year, my other big project was designing my own bar and restaurant with a different partner, also in Mexico, where I was living half the year. The challenge was to create the best bar and lounge our little town had ever seen and to meet some of the town's social and dining needs. I designed a space that was inviting and comfortable, which I'd had many years of practice doing for myself, a place where people still come to sit and socialize, have drinks and food and listen to live music six years later.

I'm no longer running the business, but the design and concept were solid and have withstood the test of time as the bar is still successfully one of the most popular venues in town. I thoroughly enjoyed the process of the design from start to finish, and I feel proud of my contribution to that town's social structure and sense of community.

Besides these few larger projects, I've also shared my passion for design over the years with my friends and family. I absolutely love helping others transform their space into something that feels like it has a cohesive design, one that is welcoming, stylish, inviting, and comforting. I think most people know what they like and what feels good to them, but they can't always translate that into a well-designed space. That's where I come in. I help them define their style and pull it all together into a cohesive design.

I've thought many times about turning this passion into a career, but I'm fortunately in a position of no longer needing to have a full-time vocation so I choose to continue to do this purely for the enjoyment and satisfaction it brings me. It warms my heart that nearly every person close to me can say they have a part of me in their homes, whether through objects I've passed along, things I've gifted, ideas or input on design, or projects I've personally helped them with.

Lil' Red

Helping those I care about in this way not only makes me feel good about my contribution to their sense of security and enjoyment of their homes, but it has also been therapeutic and healing for me, as well. Caring for my pack is a key part of who I am.

Part Four: The She-Wolf

Chapter 24

Her Pack

THOSE OF US WHO moved around a lot growing up know this to be true – home is where the heart is. Home doesn't have to be just one physical place, it's something we build up inside and around ourselves. It's our family, those born to us and those we've chosen, and our community. Whether you call it your tribe, your pack, your posse, your inner circle, or your crew— you've got to have one.

It can be large or small, friends or family, near or far. It's about creating that connection, the closeness and intimacy that provides you with a sense of belonging, support, encouragement, and personal growth. Growing up as "military brats," we were never around extended family for very long and didn't have the opportunity to establish those roots. Because we moved every couple of years, I learned very quickly that I did better when I could make at least one or two good friends in each place we lived, knowing we would only be there for a year or two at most. But while I was living in any given place, it was important to me to plant even the smallest of roots. Having a close friend, a confidant, a comrade, and someone to trust was critical to my assimilation into a new place. It helped me feel grounded there, wherever *there* was.

I applied this principle to the places I lived as an adult, as well. When I first settled in Boulder, Colorado, just after I broke free from my abusive marriage, I was in the process of healing from that abuse so the connections I sought there weren't social, they were more pragmatic. I wasn't a resident at the safehouse in Boulder, but I did participate in their outreach program where I connected on a very deep level with a group of women who had a shared experience—they were also survivors of domestic violence. Surrounding myself with those women was critical at that time, since only they could empathize. They had a full understanding of what I had been through, how I felt, and what I needed to recover and heal. I was in private therapy sessions, as well, but participating in the group sessions was one of the smartest choices I made. It became one of the most powerful parts of my healing journey. Those women gave me perspective, support, validation, and feedback that I wouldn't have had otherwise.

Once I moved to a small town nearby and settled down to build a family, I carefully curated a group of close friends, most of whom I met through my daughters' activities or their school. I dubbed our group of about ten friends the "Ya-Yas" after reading the book, *The Divine Secrets of the Ya-Ya Sisterhood*. That group would prove to be a critical source of support and joy over the course of my twenty years in that neighborhood.

We watched one another's children, we helped each other with home projects, took fun trips together, had frequent social gatherings, counseled, grew together, and provided love, friendship, and encouragement for one another over the years. As our children all grew and our lives shifted and evolved, the connections did, too. But those years, those moments, helped shape who I am today, and I will forever be grateful for them.

While living in Mexico for several years, I created another pack there. Those connections looked and felt different from my Colorado pack since those friendships weren't born out of shared experiences, but the core connections were the same – the camaraderie, support, encouragement, and especially the social engagements. We often had beach days together or gathered at one of our homes for a meal, laughter, and long hours of sharing details of our lives. We played board games together and even enjoyed live music at a local bar or sang karaoke together. Even though I've now moved away and moved on, I value the friendships I forged there and the memories of countless good moments shared.

My most important pack, the family pack, I take everywhere with me in my heart. They are with me always, everywhere I go. It includes my husband, my three daughters, my sister, and extended family, both chosen and in-law. As a she-wolf, I am fiercely loyal and protective of this pack. They mean the world to me. They are part of me. I would defend them with my life, do anything for them, and I know they all feel the same.

I would never abandon them. I am always there for them, as they are for me. I love them unconditionally. Nothing in life matters more to me than my family pack.

Chapter 25

Her Cubs

I'D WANTED TO BE A mother since I was six years old. Many young girls have the same feeling, but I *really* knew it. It went beyond just playing with dolls, it was something deep inside of me. Of course, I also wanted to be a hairdresser and teacher, too, but mostly I wanted to be a mom.

Considering my traumatic experiences as a child, the abuse I suffered from my own mother and the absence of an example of good mothering, it may seem surprising I would even want kids of my own. But I knew deep down I was born to be a mother. After the painful loss of my twins when I was nineteen, I wondered if it would still happen someday and held out hope that it would. I told myself the time hadn't been right then, that they were better off not being born into the life of violence I was living at the time. But the loss of my twins left a hole in my heart and would always be sad.

Years after I escaped that situation, I found myself married to a gentle, kind, loving man, and knew my first order of business was to start a family. My husband was

Part Four: The She-Wolf

equally intent, so we started "trying" shortly after our wedding. It took nearly a year, which seemed strange considering how, only a few years earlier, I'd unexpectedly gotten pregnant while on the pill. But come September, I was finally pregnant, with a due date just after my own birthday in April.

I was off to a rocky start, with intense morning sickness and throwing up nearly every fifteen minutes, so I was forced to take a month off from work. During that time, I received IVs once a week for dehydration. The frequency lessened, but I continued to have morning sickness each day until my first daughter was born.

Despite the physical challenges, I was beyond thrilled to be pregnant. I was sure this time would be different and was so relieved when I made it past the four-month mark. My life was distinctly different than it was during my first pregnancy. This time, I had a loving, supportive partner, a good life and a safe home. I was finally going to break the cycle of abuse. I was going to be the best mother I could be.

Although I had done all the work of healing after the abusive relationship, some of the residual fear re-surfaced when I was pregnant in the form of nightmares. I found myself dreaming that my ex-husband had found me and was either threatening me or taking away my baby. Even though I sought counseling again, to try to resolve these feelings, the nightmares and fear of him resurfacing would continue for several years finally just resolving itself with time.

Everything I had experienced as a child compelled me to mother my own child in a completely different way than what I had known growing up. Since I didn't have a good example to follow, I decided I'd just do the opposite of what I had experienced and I knew I had a lot to learn.

But these things I knew:

- My child would know she was loved—unconditionally. I would tell her every day.
- My child would believe in herself. I would assure her she was good enough, help her to learn from her mistakes, and support her be the best versions of herself. I would tell her, "You're great. You can do *anything*. I believe in you."
- My child would be not just accepted for who she is but *celebrated*. I would not try to make her into what I thought she should be, I would celebrate her unique qualities.
- My child would feel safe. I would learn other ways of discipline that encouraged self-growth and self-regulation, and I would never lay a hand on her.
- My child would feel heard and seen. I would listen to her, talk with her, and enjoy just being with her.
- My child would be reassured, cuddled, and held tight. There would be consistent affirmations and positive reinforcement.
- My child would learn that it's okay to make mistakes. I would teach her that we're all human, that as long as we learn from our mistakes and use that to grow, then it's not a waste. And when she makes poor choices, she's not a bad person. It's bad *behavior*.

Part Four: The She-Wolf

Having an insecure childhood can limit how you think about yourself and what you believe you are capable of. It pushes you to search for what you didn't have, rather than focus on what you could be. While I did spend a large part of adulthood searching for the unconditional love, acceptance, and approval I didn't receive as a child, somehow, I still believed I could do anything, be anything.

It had to have been my fuck-you gene at work, that resilience, tenacity, and strong will that I had worked so hard to cultivate. Maybe some of it came from my Irish ancestors, right along with my red hair—they're a tough lot! Whatever it was, it's the thing that still today allows me to believe in myself and be anything or do anything I set my mind to.

And what I wanted to be then was a great mother. I didn't want to just be a better mother than mine was. I wanted to be the best mother I could be. I devoured all the books I could get my hands on about being pregnant and what to expect, about child development, and any discipline methods that didn't involve spanking.

I found that, once my beautiful daughters were born, mothering came naturally and easily to me. I had good, nurturing instincts and followed them. Having a solid, present, and supportive partner made all the difference. I was living my dream. I did all the things I set out to do as a mother and more.

Another big part of my determination to break the cycle of violence was my commitment to higher education. Reading and learning about parenting and discipline was a good start, but I wanted to pursue a college degree. I had seen what happened to my mother when she divorced my dad after twenty years of marriage, having been a full-time mom all those years with no formal education or skills. While I believed strongly that the choice of being a full-time mother was important to me as well, I also felt that I needed to have a college degree to fall back on should I ever need it.

Since I had wanted to be a teacher for as long as I had wanted to be a mother, I chose elementary education as my field of study. My goal was to get a bachelor's degree in liberal arts with a teaching certification.

Although my father had attended university, he hadn't completed his degree. Instead, he chose to enlist in the army to serve his country and start a family. My sister attended college for a couple of years, as well, but didn't end up completing her degree, either. My brother served briefly in the army after high school but then moved on to the life of an artist and musician in Europe. So I would be the first and only person in my family to receive a degree. This mattered a great deal to me, and I was determined to make it a reality.

Anyone who knows me is fully aware that I have a "tendency" for impatience, but my pursuit of a college degree is a fitting example of my determination and tenacity. It took me ten years to get my diploma, going eight years part-time and the last two years full-time. I didn't let the fact that we couldn't afford even community college tuition get in my way. I wrote a short essay and was awarded a grant from the state that covered all my core courses. By the time I switched over to full-time at Regis University, eight years later, I was able to afford the full tuition.

My daughters were all very young at the time, so I spent my days as a full-time mother and my nights, after they

Part Four: The She-Wolf

went to bed, as a student. A good portion of my courses were centered around child development, which was well-aligned with my pursuit of becoming a better parent. In fact, I'd say that having a full understanding of the stages of development and what behavior to expect at each stage was, for me, the most useful knowledge I acquired during those years. It provided me with realistic expectations for my children's behavior and allowed me to respond to their behavior accordingly.

We set out to teach our three children respect, that you give it and get it back in return. We taught them that it's okay to challenge authority or the status quo, as long as you do it with respect. They learned how to be self-disciplined, to decipher right from wrong, and to be well-behaved because it was the right thing to do, not out of fear. We spent many hours listening to and talking with them, building them up, encouraging them to be independent thinkers. We worked hard to make them feel heard, safe, and loved unconditionally, no matter what.

We taught them that having poor judgement or bad behavior didn't make you a bad person, that as long as we learn from our mistakes, nothing is a waste. Once they were older, in their teens, I even joked with them, saying that I was human, too, and far from perfect. I assured them everything I did was out of love and I was doing the best I could. I confessed I was likely making mistakes and would gladly pay for their therapy later in life if they needed it.

As part of our decision to be fully present for our kids, we agreed when my first daughter was born that I would quit my job and be a full-time mother. The choice was easy for me, since this was something I'd always wanted and looked forward to. Making that dream a reality was a little harder, though. It took conscious effort and deliberate choices on our part. We spent less on vacations and travel. We had nice, but not new cars. We lived in an adequate home, nothing fancy, and we cooked at home rather than eating out. We didn't really see these things as sacrifices but rather the choices we made in order make our dream life a reality. We lived within our means and didn't build up debt or live on credit. As much as society tempted us to stray from our plan, we persevered, because it was important to us. Me staying home with our girls was our priority.

In addition to following through on all the vows I made to myself and my children on how to raise them, providing them with a safe, loving home was key in helping them to realize their inner strength and belief in themselves, fortifying them the same way I had done for myself for so many years.

Chapter 26

Her Courage

A SHE-WOLF HAS THE courage to face her fears, to confront her past, and to embrace forgiveness.

Forgiveness is letting go of the hope of a different past.

We can't change the past. We can only change how we choose to move through it, and what we decide to carry with us.

Forgiveness means different things to different people. It can look and feel different from one situation to the next, from one relationship to another. I've had many situations throughout life when I've had to make a choice to forgive someone, in some instances for some very serious, deep wounds. Part of my journey of healing from the abuse I suffered was to consider forgiveness in each situation and ask myself not just can I forgive this person, but do I have to forget to forgive? Will it make me weaker and more vulnerable? Or will it actually make me stronger? And the big question, how will the other person respond or react to me digging up past grievances?

A few years after I'd escaped my abusive marriage, managed to get a divorce, and successfully created a new, better life for myself, I was participating in a group therapy session at the safehouse near me where I also volunteered as a Victim's Advocate. I had been attending sessions about once a month for nearly a year.

During one particular session, the therapist opened up a discussion about forgiveness. It was a deeply moving, heated debate, charged with emotions from all sides of the argument. Many felt their abusers didn't deserve forgiveness, *ever*. Some said they could forgive but would never forget. There was even one woman who said she thought her abuser should pay the ultimate price of death, for what he'd done.

The therapist proposed that the anger we carried around did more damage to us than to anyone else. She stated that, when we held onto anger and resentment, it would only fester within us. She suggested we shouldn't wait for our abusers to *ask* for forgiveness and that, realistically, most of them probably never would. We should do it for ourselves and no one else.

I was caught off guard when, about a year after my divorce, Larry sent me a ten-page handwritten letter in which he shared stories of his own abuse by his stepmother, as a child and young adult. Even though he didn't outright admit to any wrongdoing toward me, I felt like he was attempting to apologize by way of explanation. After the group therapy meeting, I reflected on that letter, my life with him, all the pain he'd caused me and the possibility of forgiving him. I agreed with the therapist's claim that the

Part Four: The She-Wolf

anger and resentment I felt toward him was absolutely holding me back. Not only was I mired down in those feelings of anger and resentment, but they were also keeping me from opening up to any new relationships.

I talked it over at length with a couple of close, trusted friends and they emphatically agreed that it was time for me to forgive Larry. He didn't ask for it, maybe he didn't even deserve it, but *I* needed it. I had done so much work already—getting free of him, securing a divorce, rebuilding my life in a new place, and had participated in individual and group therapy. This was the crucial last piece of the puzzle. I needed to finally let go completely.

My two girlfriends and I devised a plan. They agreed to go with me on a drive, up Boulder Canyon to a spot where we could park and hike down to the riverbank. I took his letter with me, and as we stood there, with the river rushing by, I closed my eyes, crumpled each page into a ball one by one, and took a deep breath. I envisioned Larry and summoned up the painful memory of years of suffering. Then, with tears in my eyes, I tossed it *all* into the river.

As I threw it, I shouted, "*I forgive you!*" The physical motion of releasing that crumpled letter, combined with the mental vision was incredibly powerful. This method of physically releasing pain and trauma is something I have repeated many times throughout my life, and it is always intensely moving and freeing.

My next big opportunity for forgiveness came several years later. When I was only thirty-two, my dad died at the young age of fifty-nine from colon cancer. His illness and death drove me to dive deep into my childhood memories. He was diagnosed with aggressive stage 4 cancer on my thirty-first birthday, a phone call I'll never forget. He had

Lil' Red

surgery shortly after and then died a year and half later, after a long, difficult, painful battle.

During that year, I made it a point to spend as much time as I could with him, even though it meant going back and forth from Colorado to Arizona, often with my three young girls in tow. He did manage to make the trip to Colorado once to visit us during that time, as well. I realized I had to decide which of my grievances with him I would try to resolve and which I would let go.

In a stolen quiet moment after my daughters had gone to sleep, I shared with him how he had failed me in a time when I needed him most. I expressed how painful it was for me that he hadn't been there for me after I'd moved away and gotten married, when I was suffering the abuse and especially, the miscarriage.

He'd actually called me, coincidentally while I was in the hospital after it happened, because it had been on my birthday. I'd told him what had happened during that call, but he'd only said what everyone else around me was saying—that it was God's will, that it wasn't meant to be, and things would be okay. Definitely not what I needed to hear, and I certainly didn't feel like he was stepping up to defend me or try to protect me in that moment.

He hadn't reached out to me, supported me, or helped me get out of my situation. The worst part was, when I finally came to him for help and sought refuge with him in Idaho, he deflected and pushed me off on my grandmother. Then, he chose to enable my abuser to find me again by disclosing my location to him and then arranged a meeting in an effort to mediate.

My dad listened as I shared my grievances, and then I gave my dad the opportunity to explain things from his point of view. He shared how he'd been personally struggling for years. He'd divorced my mom, met and married his new wife, retired from the army after twenty years of service and was struggling to transition to work in the private sector. He had been having marital problems and ended up divorcing his second wife and he'd moved from Idaho to Arizona for a new job shortly before his cancer diagnosis. Seeing all of it from his perspective and understanding what he was going through, while allowing room for his humanness, helped me reach a point where I could forgive him.

My friend, Christine, once said, "Everything in life is either a problem to solve or a truth to accept." There were things I chose not to delve into with him, things I will always wonder about, like why he and my mom moved to the small apartment when I was sixteen with no bedroom for me. That is something I will never understand or condone. Those are hard truths that I have had to accept. They are part of my past and part of the building blocks that make me who I am today.

After my dad's death, I found out he had done some other things I didn't know about while he was alive, things that brought me more pain. He had never offered to support me in any way to pursue higher education. He had never given me any financial support, let alone the emotional support I needed. When I found out he had given all of those things to his second wife's son, it hurt deeply. And since he'd died by then, I would never have the chance to get an explanation or to reach some kind of understanding.

It took me many years to finally let go of this pain, too. In the end, I decided it wasn't something I could change and that holding onto the hope of a different past wasn't serving me, so I let it go and forgave him. I wrote it out on paper, how it made me feel, how I didn't understand it but had to accept it, and then I threw it in the river. I let go of the past I couldn't change and made room for forgiveness and peace.

Working through the issues with my father before his death naturally led me to a point of processing through my past with my mother. It wasn't until after my father died that I fully considered the abuse and abandonment by my mother. At that time, my relationship with her was strained, but we were making a concerted effort to stay connected.

I was living in Colorado, and she was still in Washington, recovering from the trauma of the sudden death of her second husband a few years earlier. I was trying to involve her in my daughters' lives by taking them to visit her or having her out to Colorado for visits with us. She'd even been present for the birth of my youngest daughter, which was something I never thought would happen, for her to be connected to me in such an intimate way.

On one of those visits, I had the opportunity to bravely begin the conversation with her about the abuse. She had seen how I disciplined my girls and commented on the absence of using physical force (she referred to it as *spanking*) but noting how effective my disciplinary methods were. I asked her about the way she'd abused me, why she hit me, calling it "excessive force," and gave her a chance to tell me her perspective.

She explained how she had been treated by her own mother, growing up, and that control through physical force was all she knew. She told me about how it felt, being in her early twenties and having three young kids so close in age, with my dad away at war and then later gone so

Part Four: The She-Wolf

often with his army training exercises. She said she felt she had done the best she could, but she admitted that how she disciplined me was different from that of my sister and brother. She admitted that, with me, she had felt angrier toward me and she knew it was unfair and excessive. She said she didn't even really know why she'd been that way, but expressed that she was sorry for it.

That acknowledgment, admission, and apology became one of the most powerful moments of my life.

I didn't condone her behavior. I didn't accept it or forget it. In fact, I rejected it and chose to create a different legacy with my own children. But I had a new understanding that did help me forgive her. She didn't *ask* me to forgive her, it was something I did for myself.

Having children of my own helped me to see her life in a different light. I could empathize with her struggles as a young mother. I do wish I'd gone a step further and sought to resolve my issues of abandonment with her, as well, but I didn't. Just a few short years later, when I felt that her relationship with me was still verbally and emotionally abusive and detrimental to my mental health, I decided, for my own sake, to break off our relationship completely. So again, it seems I'll never get the satisfaction of an explanation or understanding of the reasons behind her and my father's actions. Another truth to accept, another hope of a different past to let go of.

An amazing thing happened after I addressed the many years of child abuse with my mother and the issues with my father and then found my way to forgiveness with them. The heaviness of the anger and resentment I felt toward them was replaced with a lightness, optimism, and positivity. It was such an incredible feeling.

Shortly after the breakthrough with my mother, I was talking with my brother by phone and shared with him the difficult truth of my experience growing up, the extent of the abuse. I explained that I knew my experience was different from his and my sister's. I told him about how I'd talked through it with our mother and how she'd shared with me about her background, her own experiences and trauma as a child and that she'd ended up apologizing to me.

His reaction shocked me. I hadn't stopped to think about how he might react, that he might reject my truth. He became very defensive of her and began yelling at me, accusing me of trying to destroy our family by telling lies and creating drama where there wasn't any.

"Why would you do that? What is the matter with you?" he yelled.

I argued back, making efforts to defend myself. I even pointed out that she had agreed and apologized.

"Why would she do that if it weren't true?" I asked.

He insisted I had pressured her, forced her, and that she'd only done it out of guilt, maintaining it was all manufactured lies. I ended the call stating that, if he truly felt that way, then I couldn't talk to him anymore. All the pain I'd suffered was bad enough, but to have him accuse me of lying on top of it all was just too much.

We didn't talk again for twenty years.

Writing it now, it seems so extreme. But he and I hadn't been close for a long time. We were already estranged for other reasons and this was the proverbial "icing on the cake."

Part Four: The She-Wolf

About twenty years later, I went with my sister to visit him on his deathbed at the young age of forty-nine, in the south of France where he had lived most of his adult life. I was able to talk through that conversation with him, and we both found some peace. I found the words I'd desperately searched for twenty years prior, and I reassured him that just because my experience was different from his, it didn't diminish, change, or invalidate his. His experiences, his memories were still intact.

I assured him that our memories didn't have to be the same to be real. They couldn't possibly *all* be the same, anyway. And it didn't mean I didn't have a multitude of good memories, good experiences, and things that I was grateful for that I'd gained from our parents. I assured him that we did have some shared memories, too, and that the bad memories don't erase the good.

The good moments are still there, and over time, I've learned to focus on the good, to reflect with understanding, and to forgive the bad. And that's what I did then—I forgave him. It felt good. I wish it had been for a different reason, but I'm forever grateful it happened at all and that he didn't die without us having had the chance to reconcile.

That doesn't mean there aren't scars left behind from the pain and trauma of my childhood abuse. Those scars are there to remind me of what I've been through, the adversity I've overcome in life in order to become who I am now. Still to this day, so many years later, reflecting on my past brings tears to my eyes. I do wish Lil' Red hadn't experienced the pain of rejection, loss, abandonment, and physical and mental abuse. I wish she hadn't suffered years of bullying. But I can't wish that past away for her, nothing can erase it.

Lil' Red

All I can do is face it, understand it, work all the way through it, and free myself of it.

We can't change the past. We can only change how we choose to move through it, what we can learn from it, and then go beyond it.

We don't always get to choose the moments in life that make us who we are.

Lil' Red didn't choose ridicule and abuse.
She didn't choose pain and suffering.
Life had other plans for her.
She did what she had to – she grew stronger, fought back, broke free, rose above it, and kept going.

There were times when it felt like the pain would swallow her whole, pull her under.

She ultimately turned moments to memories, pain and suffering to lessons, and knowledge to wisdom.

Life would continue to have its ups and downs, its hardships, even more wolves.

She would continue to dig deep, calling on her fuck-you gene, her grit, determination, and resilience, when she needed it.

She wouldn't just make lemonade from lemons (or margaritas from limes). She would create a full, beautiful life by surrounding herself with her pack and the love she always sought and had learned to give.

She would continue to build den after den, finally making her way to the beach, creating her ultimate sanctuary with her partner in life.

Part Four: The She-Wolf

She would continue to persevere through life's challenges with a new partner by her side.

She is now me.

I *am* the She-Wolf

Lil' Red

PART FIVE
Let's Talk More About It

"To know even one life has breathed easier because you have lived, that is to have succeeded."
– Ralph Waldo Emerson

Lil' Red

Part Five: Let's Talk More About It

Part 1 – The Little Wolves

Bullying

IN PART 1, I REVISITED my experiences as a child, growing up as a military "brat," moving every couple of years, not fitting in, and being bullied by the *little wolves*. Some of the main takeaways regarding childhood bullying are as follows:

- Bullying is about their pain and trauma, not yours.
- They want to put you down to make themselves feel better, but it only works if you let them. They're the ones with low self-esteem and no self-worth, trying to transfer it to you.
- They work to gain "followers" to build themselves up, work against you as a group, exclude you from group activities, or shun/ostracize you socially.
- Bullying is when one intentionally uses words or actions against someone to cause distress to a group or individual.

- We need to teach tolerance and kindness in schools, teach kids how to express themselves and give bullies a voice.
- Child bullies haven't learned other ways of getting what they want. They learn that they can control and manipulate others through bullying and often grow into adult bullies. They are at risk for aggressive behavior toward their spouse and their own children, perpetuating the cycle. This is a cycle we absolutely need to break. Early intervention is key for eradicating domestic violence.
- We need to incorporate more anti-bullying and zero tolerance of bullying behavior in schools as the standard, build "Communities of Respect," and help kids learn how to express themselves in other ways.
- We should arm kids with non-violent ways to deal with bullies.
- We can arm bullies with skills to voice their insecurities, express their pain, build them up, and validate their worth.

Part 2 - The Mama & Papa Wolves

Parental Abuse

IN PART 2, WE WALKED back through my childhood and my connections, or lack of, with extended family, as well as my own parents. I shared the impact their abusive form of punishment had on me throughout the years and how it affected me, both as a child and through adulthood. I also shared how I experienced lack of attachment, safety, and security, as well as abandonment. The main points I highlighted are:

Expectations

- All parents could benefit from learning about the stages of development of children, to help give them realistic expectations of kids' behavior at different stages.

- Non-violent discipline teaches children self-control and self-discipline, and it promotes positive self-esteem and a strong sense of self-worth.

- Non-violent discipline guides behavior through positive reinforcement, clear and realistic expectations, logical/appropriate consequences, and open, respectful communication.

Accept Them for Who They Are

- Accepting children for who they are is crucial to their security and self-worth. Oftentimes it's just a matter of changing up how we think about different character traits. The difference is in how we see them, whether in a positive or negative light.

For example:

- The positive side of what we call stubbornness in kids is self-awareness, confidence, or tenacity. Stubbornness is also a sign of being self-assured and decisive. These are great qualities, whether in an adult or child.

- Defiance in a child is later hailed as someone who pushes boundaries, questions the status quo, is an innovator, and demonstrates strong personal conviction.

- What is considered impulsive in a child, is recognized in adulthood as someone who is decisive, spontaneous, and adventurous.

- A child deemed as reckless is later seen as someone who isn't afraid to try things, someone who takes risks and thinks "outside the box," an innovator.

- Spirited or strong-willed kids like Lil' Red are later considered to be confident, capable, fearless, resilient, and tenacious.

Part Five: Let's Talk More About It

Identifying character traits in our children, looking at them in a more positive light, and then nurturing, encouraging, and celebrating them is so much healthier than demeaning, disregarding, shaming, and denigrating them.

Part 3 - The Big, Bad Wolf

Domestic Violence

IN PART 3 - THE BIG, Bad Wolf, I shared my journey through a loving, supportive relationship that devolved into a violent, abusive, destructive marriage. By retelling those events and experiences, I hoped to provide some insight into the thoughts and feelings, hardship, pain, and trauma experienced by a victim of abuse (physical, mental, and emotional).

The signs listed below can provide assistance in identifying abusive behavior in your own relationship or that of others around you. I also shared my strategies for coping, recovery, and therapy that I engaged in, not just to survive but to thrive!

Red Flags

Red flags are similar to warning signs, but they differ in the ways they can present themselves early on in a relationship. Each can be a sign that there may be a Big Bad Wolf lurking underneath a facade of charm, humor, affection, and love.

Part Five: Let's Talk More About It

- While dating, they want to monopolize your time, encouraging you to spend less time with family and friends, to focus only on them.
- They start to become your only source of influence. *They* are the only ones building you up, lavishing you with affection to the point where there's no room for anyone else.
- They act differently when they're just with you and are not the same person as they are when around others, not even necessarily in a bad way. They are often charming, engaging, or the life of the party. Then, they become critical and controlling when alone with you, sort of the "Jekyll and Hyde" persona.
- They always tell you what you want to hear—never contradict you, offer insights, play devil's advocate, or offer another point of view.
- They never take accountability for their own actions—everything is always someone else's fault.
- They encourage physical isolation from family or friends. Abuse, control, and manipulation thrive in isolation, where they are free to exert their power.
- They never get angry. If someone never shows their anger or frustration, you can't know how they will manage it in the future, especially in trying times.
- They engage in putting down or belittling others to impress you (like in a restaurant to a server), or being cruel to animals or children.

- They ignore boundaries, offer excuses as to why but continue to do so.

The presence of these traits doesn't automatically mean someone will be abusive. These are just red flags, common character traits of abusers. So, be aware and go with caution.

Warning Signs

Here are some warning signs of abusive behavior. If you notice these in your own relationship or that of someone you know, urgently consider making a change. At a minimum, seek counsel from someone you trust or one of the many organizations created that support victims of abuse.

- Disrespect: It's common for an abusive partner to make derogatory, demeaning, or shaming remarks about you, not just in private but in front of others, as well.

- Manipulation: Abusers are master manipulators. They use anger and intimidation, even threats to frighten and control you.

- Withholding affection or attention: A controlling partner will withhold affection or intimacy to manipulate you and as punishment for not being compliant to their will.

- Blame: An abuser will blame you for their anger and abuse and other things that are *their* fault.

- Cycle of conflict: In an abusive relationship, there's a repetitive cycle of minor issues that become conflict, which escalates to an outburst of verbal or physical abuse (sometimes both), remorse, reconciliation, and then withdrawal.

- Threats: Someone who is abusive will use gestures, intimidation of physical size, shouting, weapons, or verbal threats.

- Jealousy: Extreme jealousy is a sign of insecurity, but an abuser will argue that it is out of love, questioning who you spend time with, falsely accusing you of infidelity, and possibly restricting your activities as a means of controlling your interactions with others.

Part 4 - The She-Wolf

Strong and Resilient

IN PART 4, I EXPLORED how I became the She-Wolf, strong, determined, and resilient. This is a summary of those main ideas, including things you can do yourself in order to bring out your own inner She-Wolf.

Breaking the Cycle of Violence

- Use non-violent discipline with your children.
- Give unconditional love, through consistent and continual reassurance.
- Help your child to believe in themselves and learn from their mistakes. Allow them to be human.
- Accept your child as they are. Do not make them into what you think they should be. Celebrate their unique qualities.
- Give your child a safe, loving, supportive environment. Teach them self-growth and self-discipline.
- Do not engage in physical discipline at all.

Part Five: Let's Talk More About It

- Teach mutual respect.
- Listen to your children, acknowledge their feelings and express them, and talk with them daily about anything.
- Enjoy just being with your children. Have realistic expectations for age-appropriate behavior.

Building Up Your Resilience, Fortifying Yourself

- Create comfortable, inviting, safe spaces for yourself.
- Clean out your emotional "closet." Do the work to go through past pain and trauma, and come out the other side of it. Otherwise, it just builds up inside you and festers, creating a multitude of emotional and even physical problems.
- Forgive past grievances, even if just for yourself. Don't wait for someone else to ask.
- Find the Lil' Red inside of you. When you face hardships, dig down deep. Find your determination, grit, resiliency, your "fuck-you" gene, and tap into it. Get some *Reditude*!
- Take action—do the things you know you need to do, reach out for help. Make small shifts by doing a little less of *this*, a little more of *that*. Keep at it until you get to a better place.
- Cultivate your own extended family, a close circle of friends whom you trust, those who inspire and uplift you, help and encourage you to be your best self.

Final Thoughts and Affirmations

> Abuse has nothing to do with *YOU*.
> It has everything to do with *THEM*.
> It has to do with their pain and trauma.
> It has to do with how they're choosing to cope.
> It's all about them, not *YOU*.
> They're trying to make their pain your pain. Don't let them.
> They're trying to break you, manipulate and control you. Don't let them.
> You *CAN* heal from the pain, you *CAN* love yourself again, and you *CAN* trust again.
> You have to grieve the loss and let go of the hope for a different past. Forgive them and forgive yourself.
> You have to grieve the loss of the future you thought would happen.
> You have to reframe and rebuild your life.

If you or someone you know feel that you are being abused, *reach out for help*. You can call the Domestic Violence Hotline (800) 799-7233, or reach out to a local shelter for immediate assistance or outreach support.

You can contact one of the many other organizations created to support victims of abuse. Reach out to those around you whom you trust, even if you have to keep telling your story over and over until you're heard.

Get out if you aren't safe—there are places you can go, people who can help and protect you.

Part Five: Let's Talk More About It

Everyone deserves a safe environment, free from physical, mental, and emotional abuse, to be unharmed by those we trust and lead a life free of control and manipulation. We all deserve to be free to be *human*, to make mistakes and learn from them, to grow, experience, and be in the world in the way that makes sense to us.
Everyone.

Acknowledgments

I'VE OFTEN WONDERED, over the years, if telling the story of my experiences with bullying, abuse, and domestic violence as a child and young adult might be beneficial to anyone. I decided, after conquering a nearly two-year long battle with an autoimmune disease and a significant birthday looming, the time was right. I realized I needed to tell the story for *myself*, that I would benefit personally from the deep dive into my past more than anyone.

I want to thank my husband, Jake, for showing me unconditional love and unwavering support in all that I do, but especially for making me feel safe and loved throughout this process.

I am also grateful to my writing coach and friend, Raina O'Dell, for her support, encouragement, and guidance through this process and for inspiring me with her own writing and fearless pursuit of living her best life.

To the publisher, Samantha Joy, who serves as an example of how a strong, capable woman with a tender heart can also be wildly powerful and successful.

To my daughters, who have inspired me to break the cycle of violence, to be the best mother I could be, and to be my best self in all things. Their unconditional love and

Acknowledgments

acceptance have fortified me more deeply than I could ever have imagined.

Special thanks to my sister, Kellie, for being willing to walk back through childhood events and memories to provide clarification when I needed it, for her constant support and encouragement, and for protecting and caring for Lil' Red as best she could.

And to my chosen sister, Elizabeth, for being a beta reader, providing valuable input from the heart and being a sounding board whenever I needed it. Her special way of guiding, supporting, encouraging, and celebrating alongside me is invaluable.

Lastly, I want to thank my parents for all that I learned from them and for all the gifts they shared that have made me who I am today.

About the Author

JILL SAFARI IS A MOTHER, wife, artist, author, and survivor of child abuse, bullying and domestic violence. Over the years, she has worn many hats with her most rewarding and important role being a full-time mother to her three incredible daughters. She has also been a teacher, a business owner, and a volunteer and mentor in her community.

Her life experience, coupled with her education and passion for helping others, has led her to this current chapter in life. She has chosen to share her personal story, her own experiences with abuse, in the hope of shedding light on these issues as well as creating awareness for others. It is her belief that sharing from her point of view will give insights into a victim's thoughts and feelings, along with some of the behavior and patterns that are red flags. She examines behavior our society should deem unacceptable and ways of coping with and healing from abuse. Her life is proof that the cycle of violence can be broken, and you can not only survive, but thrive!

www.ingramcontent.com/pod-product-compliance
Lightning Source LLC
LaVergne TN
LVHW011417080426
835512LV00005B/107

9781959955603